Philosophers
Look at
Science Fiction

Philosophers Look at Science Fiction

NICHOLAS D. SMITH, editor

Nelson-Hall nh Chicago

LIBRARY OF CONGRESS CATALOGING IN PUBLICATION DATA
Main entry under title:

Philosophers look at science fiction.

  Includes bibliographical references and index.
  1. Science fiction, American — History and criticism — Addresses, essays, lectures.
2. Philosophy in literature. I. Smith, Nicholas D.
PS374.S35P4 1982   813'.0876'09   82-7977
ISBN 0-88229-740-6 (cloth)   AACR2
ISBN 0-88229-807-0 (paper)

Manufactured in the United States of America

10 9 8 7 6 5 4 3 2 1

The paper in this book is pH neutral (acid-free).

I am indebted to Betty Queen Davis, Jeanne Keister, Robin Rogers, Nancy McGovern, and Robert Steele for their help in preparing and editing the manuscript.

Contents

Preface _____

In the early days of philosophy, the philosopher was construed as anyone with intellectual interests. The learned endeavor that was once generally called philosophy is today specialized in fields such as physics, mathematics, biology, sociology, political science, psychology, or any of a host of others. This is not surprising, given the meaning of the word *philosophy:* "love of wisdom." But as the various specialized fields have broken away, the remainder, philosophy, has become an increasingly misunderstood profession. As a result of this misunderstanding, those engaged in philosophy have increasingly withdrawn into the academic world, seeking audiences that share their specialized interests. This has led to a further decrease in the interest in and comprehension of the intellectual pursuits of a philosophical nature.

Another consequence of this misunderstanding is an increasing reticence among philosophers to address issues outside their narrowing fields, or to address the issues within their fields in a simple way, easily accessible to nonprofessionals. Those who do attempt to appeal to a broader audience are often viewed with suspicion by their colleagues.

Within the profession, the degree of success is often assessed largely, if not entirely, by the extent to which the philosopher in question has published his research in scholarly journals. This standard has had two effects of special interest here. First, there has been in recent years a proliferation of such journals, and the demand for space in them is far greater than the space available. But in all of this activity, the ironic fact remains that relatively few people ever read the work that is published in such journals, and in most cases those that do are other professional philosophers. But as always, philosophical questions continue to have great appeal to people with even the mildest of intellectual interests. So we come to the second effect of this standard: as philosophers continue to move into narrower and narrower areas, and to speak to more and more specialized audiences, philosophical questions are more frequently becoming the basis of work outside the profession.

One of the most interesting areas in which philosophical issues are explored outside the academic world of the professional philosopher is fiction, especially science fiction, for the nature of science fiction is such that it projects beyond known or accepted facts or theories. Still, most science fiction assumes that the universe is orderly, that this order can be exposed and exploited by rational endeavor—that man can change reality. These assumptions also lie behind much of philosophy. Man can change the social order; man can discover and exploit the natural order; man can move beyond what is now believed to be true. It has been said that philosophy begins in wonder, and some of the most wondrous fiction written is science fiction.

In this book, a number of professional philosophers move out of their academic roles and look critically at the topics and assumptions embodied in science fiction literature. They attempt to bring philosophy to bear on issues which go beyond the known, but not beyond what is reasonable. The assumptions of the science fiction writer and philosopher often coincide. The authors whose work appears in this book have applied their professional skills to the work and thoughts of science fiction writers. In this unique joining of minds, insights emerge concerning questions of universal interest: What if Einstein was wrong about faster-than-light travel? What if we were to encounter an alien race? What if there were other universes? What if we could be reincarnated? What if we radically changed the social order?

Such questions are the stuff of which intelligence is made, for at their foundation lie the most basic questions man can ask: What is our place in the universe? For what can we hope? What must we fear? What can we do to change the world and ourselves for the better? These are the questions addressed in this book.

1.

Introduction:
The Philosophical Appeal
of Science Fiction

FRED D. MILLER, JR. AND NICHOLAS D. SMITH

*Fred D. Miller and I have collaborated more than once
on the subjects of philosophy and science fiction,
including our book* Thought Probes: An Introduction to
Philosophy through Science Fiction *(Prentice-Hall,
1981). Miller and I are specialists in ancient Greek
philosophy. We met at a seminar on this topic at
Princeton in the summer of 1976. We soon discovered
that we had mutual interests in science fiction as well,
and our work together has continued since that time.*

*Miller received his doctorate from the University of
Washington in Seattle, and is now an Associate
Professor of Philosophy and Department Head at
Bowling Green State University. I am an Associate
Professor of Philosophy at Virginia Polytechnic
Institute and State University.*

Within a few decades enormous solar stations far off in outer space
will be feeding energy via microwave to human communities through-

1

out the solar system. To relieve human beings of the boredom, physical discomfort, and hazards of prolonged existence in space, computers and robots will be designed to operate such stations independently.

These machines will have to be very sophisticated, capable not only of performing routine tasks but also of responding to new and unpredictable problems. They will need to employ machine language to describe such problems and perform logical and mathematical calculations in order to solve them.

Imagine one such machine, Robot QT-1, which has just been assembled by the human beings Powell and Donovan. QT-1, which has been equipped with a metallic diaphragm for speech, surprises these humans with the announcement that it does not accept their explanation for its presence on the solar station.

Powell responds, "You're the first robot who's ever exhibited curiosity as to his own existence—and I think the first that's really intelligent enough to understand the world outside."

When the men try to explain to "Cutie" the nature of the solar system and the galaxy, the robot responds, "Do you expect me to believe any such complicated, implausible hypothesis as you have just outlined?"

The machine prefers a simpler and more elegant hypothesis to save the phenomena: The station is surrounded by a black material just beyond the viewports containing little gleaming dots. The robot retreats to meditate while the men ridicule its skepticism, but it soon returns.

> "I have spent these last two days in concentrated introspection," said Cutie, "and the results have been most interesting. I began at the one sure assumption I felt permitted to make. I, myself, exist, because I think—"
>
> Powell groaned, "Oh, Jupiter, a robot Descartes!"
>
> "Who's Descartes?" demanded Donovan.

A well-trained undergraduate in philosophy could answer this question for Donovan, and could help him respond to the robot's refutation of the hypothesis that it was made by human beings.

Cutie points out that the humans are soft and flabby, that they depend on an inefficient use of organic fuel for energy, and that they periodically pass into a coma.

I, on the other hand, am a finished product. I absorb electrical energy directly and utilize it with an almost one hundred percent efficiency. I am composed of strong metal, am continuously conscious, and can stand extremes of environment easily. These are facts which, with the self-evident proposition that no being can create another being superior to itself, smashes your silly hypothesis to nothing.

This metallic metaphysician is the creation of Isaac Asimov in "Reason," a story in his book *I, Robot.*[1] It proceeds to unveil a robot's equivalent of Descartes' ontological proof of the existence of God. Cutie's Master turns out to be the energy converter on the solar station. Asimov provides further twists on the Cartesian line, since Cutie corrects Descartes' claim that human beings are essentially reasoning beings. Powell and Donovan, who repeatedly commit the fallacies *"ad hominem"* and "appeal to authority," are especially vulnerable: "I, a reasoning being, am capable of deducing Truth from *a priori* Causes. You, being intelligent, but unreasoning, need an explanation of existence *supplied* to you, and this the Master did."

Asimov writes with a detailed knowledge of—and irreverent attitude toward—the philosophy of Descartes. His story reveals itself as an amusing critique of *a priori* rationalism. The story is of value to the discipline of philosophy because it expresses an essentially philosophical theme, stated by Powell: "You can prove anything you want by coldly logical reason—if you pick the proper postulates. We have ours and Cutie has his." Asimov's story, "Reason," is a paradigm of science fiction. To be sure, seldom is science fiction replete with explicit references to philosophers and allusions to the traditional literature. Nevertheless, the philosopher and the science fiction fan have deep common interests, a fact suggested by the testimony of many science fiction readers: "I love it for the ideas in it." In this regard science fiction differs from most popular genres of fiction such as mysteries, gothics, westerns, and teenage romances. The ideas of science fiction are the ideas of philosophy in the broad, traditional sense. Science fiction is correctly named so long as one thinks of science in the root sense of *scientia*, meaning "wisdom" or "knowing." This point has been made most eloquently by science fiction writer Kate Wilhelm: "Metaphysics attempts to discover the ultimate nature of reality, and in this sense the inner-space of science fiction is metaphysical fiction."[2] Because of the interests which typify this genre, it is only fitting that science fiction is the handmaid of philosophy.

The value of science fiction to philosophy is evident from the nature of the literature. In writing science fiction an author isolates essential and significant facts of existence by projecting what is familiar into unfamiliar contexts, while either basic facts or laws undergo modification.

This definition is easier to grasp once the genus and differentia are distinguished. First, the genus. Science fiction is fiction and, more generally, art. We shall proceed from Ayn Rand's definition of art which seems, in this case, to be most appropriate: "Art is a selective recreation of reality according to an artist's metaphysical value-judgments."[3] Art does not just replicate or represent reality. Aristotle pointed out the creative function of poetry, in the broad sense, when he contrasted it with history: History "describes the thing that has been," whereas poetry "describes the thing that might be."[4] The artist selects certain features of reality and integrates them in a projection of how the world might be. This projection in literature takes the form of plot and characterization. The process of selection is governed by certain beliefs of the artist concerning what is significant or worth including in a portrayal—beliefs which are explicit in some cases but often only implicit. For example, it is no accident that a science fiction author such as Frederik Pohl represents his space explorers as individuals haunted by neurosis, guilt, and jealousy over the infidelities of loved ones. There is an implicit assumption that these are deep and essential features of the human condition which one does not overcome by being the first to set foot on Mars or by prospecting the worlds of the alien Heechee. Consider Pohl's *Man Plus* and *Gateway*. The fact that Pohl's characters cannot affect the plot by their choices, that they are doomed from the start by their internal shortcomings, reflects deterministic assumptions about human action found in the literature of Naturalism.[5]

The manner in which science fiction portrays a utopian society is also governed by the system of values of the author. An author such as Edward Bellamy, who places the highest value on security and social welfare, presents such a society in one light in *Looking Backward;* an author such as Ira Levin, who values individual freedom, casts it in another in *This Perfect Day*. Thus the genus of science fiction gives its basic purpose: what the author takes to be essential or ethically significant aspects of the familiar are projected on a new reality.

But science fiction differs in a fascinating way from other forms of literature. All fiction operates through imaginative projection and invention in its creation of new characters and plot situations. But ordinary fiction takes for granted the context of knowledge common to author and reader. Physical facts and laws of nature familiar to them are assumed. Whether the story is set in the present or the past, the recreation occurs within a context of fact and natural law. For instance, in Margaret Mitchell's *Gone with the Wind*, it must remain a fact that the South lost the Civil War; that Rhett Butler cannot pick up Scarlet O'Hara in a TransAm; that the convention of monogamy does not, alas, leave Scarlet with the option of marrying both Rhett and Ashley; and, obviously, that all the basic laws of ballistics and thermodynamics must govern the march through Georgia.

Science fiction is differentiated from other types of fiction because it takes the further giant step of assuming that these "givens" are open to modification. Most frequently, science fiction does this by introducing entities which are recognizable as homo sapiens with cultural characteristics similar to ours and projecting them into unfamiliar plot situations in the future. In this way it creates "a future in which new knowledge, new discoveries, new adventures, new mutations would make life radically different from the familiar patterns of the past and present."[6]

But science fiction is not essentially a fiction of the future. A character in the present who is presumed to possess the power of telepathy or periodic invisibility would be—and has been—a fit subject for science fiction. What is essential to science fiction is that it projects into contexts which are at variance with what is now taken to be basic fact or law. *Star Wars* is about the distant past rather than the future. It is science fiction because it projects humanlike characters into a civilization with a vastly more advanced technology than ours and into a cosmos not altogether governed by Einsteinian physics. Other science fiction works depict the consequences of some counterfactual supposition.

For example, a story is set in England in the mid-twentieth century, assuming that the Spanish Armada conquered England or that Queen Victoria was exposed as a nymphomaniac.

Our definition of science fiction implicitly ascribes an important presupposition to all forms of its literature: there is an order in the universe which can be revealed by reason. This presupposition is implied in the Aristotelian distinction between essential and accidental facts. According to Aristotle certain facts about a man like Socrates were more essential or important than others. For example, the fact that he was a rational animal was more important than that he happened to wear sandals or live in Athens. The fact that Socrates wore sandals was "accidental" in that Socrates would have remained what he was, *a man*, even if he were to exchange his sandals for a pair of cowboy boots. The idea that a person can remain *essentially* the same, while undergoing change, is important for our interpretation of science fiction.

Science fiction writers take the scientific method to be the most important or even the only legitimate way to discover the essential truths and fundamental laws of reality. This is true especially of writers and editors like Hugo Gernsbach who coined and popularized the phrase "science fiction," and John Campbell, who edited *Astounding/Analog* for decades. As a general rule, the world projected by the science fiction writer forms a coherent whole which is accessible to rational inquiry of some type.

It is possible to classify more specific forms of science fiction in terms of this definition and presupposition. Particular stories, novels, or films will clearly exemplify a given classification, but more complex works may fall under several types. Science fiction can depict worlds which are at various removes from the world as we know it; the "distance" from our world depends upon whether facts or laws are modified and upon the types of laws which are modified. We will distinguish between *natural science fiction, cultural science fiction,* and *metaphysical science fiction,* in terms of whether the work focuses on the natural laws of the physical sciences, the laws (if there are such) governing culture and social life, or the basic laws of metaphysics. We will further subdivide each of these categories into *extrapolative* and *speculative* science fiction. Extrapolative science fiction takes for granted present-day scientific and philosophical knowledge and asks, What *will* happen if this goes on? Speculative science fiction projects future developments of knowledge and asks, What *would* happen if these were to occur?

Natural science fiction refers to much of the old hardcore science fiction which appeared in the pulp magazines in the 1930s, '40s and '50s. There is a strong emphasis here on the physical sciences and biology, but not psychology.

The extrapolative natural type asks, What will happen if this goes on? It presupposes the body of scientific knowledge as it now exists but projects into an environment quite unlike the one we now experience. The simplest example of this is the host of stories, now all outdated, which projected what would happen when the first human beings landed on the moon. Others projected the first use of nuclear warfare and so forth. A more imaginative example of this sort of science fiction is Hal Clement's *Mission of Gravity*, which describes the adventures of a life form on a planet with a much stronger gravitational pull than our own. This widely respected novel carefully works out the implications of this environmental difference as to the biological structure, technology, and personal values of the myriapodal hero.

Speculative natural science fiction goes much further than this. It projects fundamental advances in future science and technology which supersede scientific theories currently in force. All stories premised upon the possibility of time travel or faster-than-light travel are of this sort. Many speculative stories will postulate one slight change and then explore in detail the ramifications of this change in terms of contemporary science. For example, Paul Anderson's *Tau Zero* projects human beings onto a spaceship which is able to accelerate at speeds close to the speed of light. The drive mechanism of the ship goes out of control through a fortuitous event, so that the ship continues to approach the speed of light and the crew members experience spectacular relativistic effects and ultimately the death and rebirth of the universe. Such speculative natural science fiction characteristically asks, What would happen if this were to be the case?[7]

Cultural science fiction focuses upon our knowledge of human culture and social life. The *extrapolative* version of cultural science fiction projects humans or intelligent life forms in unusual situations, but assumes that thought and behavior in such situations are basically explicable in terms of existing theories. A classic example of this is the film *Forbidden Planet*, in which a scientist has access to immensely powerful machinery subject to direct mental control. The results are explained in terms of the Freudian theory of the unconscious, the id, and the death wish. (This film, like some vintage hardcore science fiction films, shows one of the hazards of purely extrapolative science fiction: the "existing state of scientific knowledge," especially in human sciences like psychology, is soon out of date.)

Speculative cultural science fiction projects situations in which the social and human sciences undergo significant advances which cannot be anticipated at present. For example, Asimov's *Foundation* trilogy is premised upon the development of a science of psychohistory which can use mathematical laws to make highly accurate predictions of future collective human behavior.

Metaphysical science fiction is more unusual, especially in very speculative forms. It projects into situations in which modifications are made on the deepest levels. Perhaps the most famous example of this is A. E. Van Vogt's *World of Null-A*, which operates on the assumption that Aristotelian logic based upon the laws of identity and noncontradiction will somehow be superseded by a new, higher logic. It is not at all clear what this new logic is, but that shouldn't be too surprising. Metaphysical science fiction often employs philosophical assumptions which are quite at variance with enlightened common sense.

Some metaphysical stories work from solipsistic assumptions. Frederic Brown in "The Solipsist" questions the existence of everything until there is nothing but his mind, a fog, and the voice of God, who voluntarily vacates his place as "the only solipsist" to Brown's protagonist. Other stories work from the subjectivist assumption that reality is somehow constituted by the knowing mind. Philip K. Dick in *The Eye in the Sky* and Ursula LeGuin in *The Lathe of Heaven* have worked with this idea. Some, but not all, of the stories in this class use science in some way. The very existence of this class seems to show that science fiction does not have to involve scientific advancement or technological change.

To sum up, these varieties of science fiction isolate essential facts about human beings, conscious entities, or society, or about space, time, or cosmic history, by projecting characters into novel situations. There is a deep commitment in science fiction, as such, to the presumption that the new situations are knowable, that they are governed and rationally explicable. Absurdist, existentialist literature, the type in which human beings are inexplicably transformed into cockroaches, does not qualify as science fiction. We would include in this category P. A. Zoline's "Heat Death of the Universe" and Jorge Luis Borges' "Library of Babel," both of which depict people in absurd, irrational, nightmarish situations. However, both stories are included in Robert Silverberg's *Mirror of Infinity: A Critic's Anthology of Science Fiction,* so that by Norman Spinrad's definition of science fiction as "anything published as science fiction,"[8] they qualify. But they fail to perform a necessary function of science fiction when they presuppose that there is nothing essential, significant, or intelligible in human experience which can be represented in art. It would follow that *most* forms of fantasy which are premised on magic or the supernatural also fail to satisfy the definition of science fiction. (For an opposing viewpoint, see Justin Leiber's piece, chapter 14.)

Having defined science fiction at considerable length, it is now possible to consider how science fiction may be of service to philosophy. Science fiction as we have described it shares a fundamental goal with philosophy: the discovery of what is essential and valuable in reality. Philosophy pursues this goal with its own peculiar methodology of analysis and dialectic. Although science fiction employs the quite different techniques of fiction, it can serve as a very valuable aid to philosophy as a heuristic, diagnostic, and pedagogical tool.

Science fiction has been found to be especially useful in the classroom in enabling students to discover and appreciate philosophical issues. Sometimes the characters who are thrust into unusual situations and face new problems disagree over how to deal with the problems. This leads to dialogue that often contains explicit philosophical argument. Since the context is conversational, the argument is often more intelligible and clear than one would find in a philosophical treatise. For example, *The Moon Is a Harsh Mistress* by Robert A. Heinlein contains some interesting discussions of political and social institutions.

This novel suggests that individual freedom is a survival value, and the plot involves the revolution of freedom-loving colonists on the Moon against the authoritarian rule of Earth. A principal character, Professor De la Paz, defends a version of anarchism against the Marxist-leaning heroine, Wyoming Knott, in an argument that students find far more clear and consistent than examples drawn from the traditional philosophical literature. The argument gains urgency because it occurs in the midst of a deep political crisis. Professor De la Paz begins,

> "May I ask this? Under what circumstances is it moral for a group to do that which is not moral for a member of that group to do alone?"
> "Uh . . . that's a trick question."
> "It is the *key* question, dear Wyoming. A radical question that strikes to the root of the whole dilemma of government. Anyone who answers honestly and abides by *all* consequences knows where he stands – and what he will die for."

Wyoming challenges the professor on several points, including capital punishment. He answers,

> "I believe in capital punishment under some circumstances . . . with this difference. I would not ask a court; I would try, condemn, execute sentence myself, and accept full responsibility."
> "But – Professor, what *are* your political beliefs?"
> "I'm a rational anarchist. A rational anarchist believes that concepts such as 'state' and 'society' and 'government' have no existence save as physically exemplified in the acts of self-responsible individuals. He believes that it is impossible to shift blame, share blame, distribute blame . . . as blame, guilt, responsibility are matters taking place inside human beings singly and *nowhere else.* But being rational, he knows that not all individuals hold his evaluations, so he tried to live perfectly in an imperfect world . . . aware that his effort will be less than perfect yet undismayed by self-knowledge of self-failure."
> "Professor, your words sound good but there is something slippery about them. Too much power in the hands of individuals – surely you would not want . . . well, H-missiles for example – to be controlled by one irresponsible person?"
> "My point is that one person *is* responsible. Always. If H-bombs

exist—and they do—some *man* controls them. In terms of morals *there is no such thing as 'state.'* Just men. Individuals. Each is responsible for his own acts."

The discussion proceeds through a series of objections and responses, and Heinlein provides the professor with ample opportunity throughout the rest of the novel to expound and apply his views.

Students are challenged by the professor's argument that one's responsibility as an individual to do what is right is in no way qualified by one's membership in a group or by the orders of a superior. Most students are ultimately not convinced by his argument and try to find a way around it. Some, for example, can accept the professor's claim that one should not substitute the judgments of others, whether a leader or a group, for one's own informed moral judgment on any issue. But they argue that rational persons can agree on a set of laws and procedures for objectively applying them, even in the face of sincere disagreement.

Other students argue that the professor's methods of manipulating and coercing his "Loonie" compatriots throughout the novel are inconsistent with his own professed anarchism. But students never fail to be impressed with the professor's critique of blind obedience to the state.

This particular use of science fiction may, however, prompt an objection to our thesis. Insofar as science fiction is the handmaid of philosophy, some may feel it is didactic and therefore bad science fiction, that the author is too busy teaching philosophy to tell a story.

Heinlein's novel has, in fact, been criticized for containing too much talk and not enough action. But the philosophical passages fit well into the flow of plot, and Heinlein makes a conscious attempt to relate them to his characters' behavior. Some science fiction definitely suffers from excessive didacticism, however, and should be avoided because it bores both students and their instructors. For example, Bellamy's *Looking Backward* begins when the protagonist falls asleep and wakes up in a democratic socialist utopia in the United States at the end of the twentieth century. There the plot in effect ceases. Throughout the rest of the novel the protagonist is led from factory to factory and lectured in each factory at tedious length about the superiority of the new order to the old order. The primary purpose of science fiction is not to teach. As with any other literature, science fiction has the task of displaying abstract themes in fully concrete forms which the reader can experience. The author should not simply tell the reader that monogamy is a poor form of social life, but instead should provide the reader with the concrete experience of flesh and blood characters living in alternative systems, such as the line marriage of *The Moon Is a Harsh Mistress*.

The fact that science fiction provides concretized projections of abstract possibilities and values is important to philosophy. The wide range of this form of literature provides a rich source of fictional "case studies" or "conceptual experiments" in which it is possible to put philosophical presumptions to the test. This potential for science fiction was long ago realized by Bishop John Wilkins in *A Discourse Concerning a New World and Another Planet* (1638):

> It is my desire, that by Occasion of this Disclosure, I may raise up some more Active Spirit to search after other hidden and unknown Truths. Since it must needs be of great Impediment unto the Growth of Sciences, for Men still to Plod on upon beaten Principles as to be afraid of entertaining anything that may seem to contradict them.

Science fiction enables the student of philosophy not only to consider an alternative but to experience it in an entertaining form. There are two important ways in which science fiction can serve the purposes of philosophy. First, it has an important *aporematic*, or problem-setting, function. It can lead a student to recognize and appreciate a specific philosophical question or issue without supporting any particular solution to the problem. Second, it can have an important *persuasive* function, by leading the reader to accept one solution to a problem rather than another. Of course, mainstream fiction can also perform both functions.

Many science fiction stories are intended as puzzles or thought teasers, and these can perform the aporematic function. They can be especially useful pedagogically in the area of epistemology. Students who are unmoved at the prospect of dreaming with Descartes, of putting their hands in tepid water with Berkeley, or of walking around a table with Hume, can become excited about the skeptical problems that these philosophers were trying to illustrate when such problems have a pivotal place in an interesting science fiction story. In such a story a plausible setting is created in which what seem to be utterly justified beliefs are suddenly flung into doubt or are defeated by the unexpected appearance of incontrovertible evidence opposing those beliefs.

Because science fiction is able to project characters into radically different environments in the ways described earlier, it is uniquely suited to apply pressure to naive common sense. For example, George Henry Smith's "In the Imagicon" describes a machine that is able to create integrated experiences of imaginary worlds that are often frighteningly different from ours. The protagonist oscillates wildly between a stark, Siberian world where he is harassed by a shrew of a wife and attacked by raving carniverous beasts, and a hedonistic existence in another world of experience in which he is caressed by beautiful harem girls. It appears that he periodically escapes from the stark world via the machine into the imaginary world of the harem, but the story finally leaves the reader with the impression that the harem world is the real world, and the protagonist is trying to escape its boredom. But the ending is ambiguous: perhaps the protagonist merely *believes* that he exists in the (imaginary) harem world. Might he not in fact occupy some third world which is not even represented in the experiences Smith describes?

The problem raised in this and other stories is identical to the one raised by Descartes in the First Meditation with the old-fashioned apparatus of a *malin genie*, or evil demon, who deceives us by providing coherent worlds of fraudulent experience. Skepticism rears its head in other stories. Skepticism about memory appears in Philip K. Dick's story, "We Can Remember It for You Wholesale." Here, one can purchase utterly convincing, but false, memories.

Skepticism about the scientific method as human beings practice it is a theme of Katherine McLean's "The Trouble with You Earth People." In this story a pair of doglike extraterrestrials find humans woefully inadequate in their truthseeking methods. The human scientists believe that knowledge can only be attained through dispassionate observation and a cold-blooded and exclusively analytical methodology. The aliens find this amusing but pathetic, for their own intellectual methodology requires intense, even sexual contact between those jointly pursuing knowledge. Especially ironic is the scene in which a fastidious human scientist is fondled by an alien in its sincere and seemingly appropriate response to the human's questions about alien knowledge. Unfortunately sincerity alone cannot sustain the relationship, and contact is broken off without any significant exchange of knowledge. This is not merely presented as a problem of differing customs, for McLean's aliens are clearly represented as our intellectual superiors.

Science fiction also plays a useful problem-setting role in the areas of the philosophy of mind and philosophical anthropology when writers project the phenomenon of consciousness into new physical forms. Another robot story by Asimov entitled "Evidence" presents Stephen Byerley, a popular politician who is accused of being a robot in drag, an accusation which threatens to cost him the election to a high office. The central problem of the story involving robot psychologist Susan Calvin is how to distinguish a human being from a robot without risking the violation of a human's rights by cutting open his skull against his consent in search of a positronic robot brain. The problem is apparently solved when Byerley physically assaults a heckler, for Asimov's First Law of Robotics forbids a robot from harming a human being or allowing a human being to come to harm. Byerley wins the election and the world benefits. Yet the final lines of the story point out that the heckler struck by Byerley could have been another robot. The proposed test of humanity leads to what philosophers call an "*infinite regression,*" since we must apply the test to the heckler: was *he* a human or a robot? Clearly, it won't settle matters if the heckler is observed to strike another (human? robot?).

Asimov's story is an ingenious version of the "imitation game" described by A. M. Turing in the classic article, "Computing Machinery and Intelligence." The problem is whether there is any behavior characteristic of human beings which cannot be simulated so convincingly by a machine that we cannot tell the difference. And if there is no such behavior, is there any point to saying that human beings can "think" but machines cannot? Asimov ends his story with tongue in cheek, a character suggests, ". . . a robot might fail due to the inherent inadequacies of his brain." Ironically, this suggestion comes from the ambiguous Stephen Byerley himself.

Many other philosophical problems are posed by science fiction stories. Stories about first contact with alien life forms frequently present conflicts centering on unresolved differences in values or social ethics. How can one more memorably raise the problem of evil and thus call into question the existence of a benevolent, all-knowing, and all-powerful God than does Arthur C. Clarke in "The Star"? Here a spacefaring Jesuit discovers that a supernova has obliterated an entire sentient and admirable culture, and this supernova turns out to have been the Star of Bethlehem.

Students of philosophy can also be challenged by *persuasive science fiction,* which uses a fictional situation to make a particular thesis plausible. Academic philosophers have a good deal to learn from persuasive science fiction. Several decades ago philosophers were deploying "ordinary language arguments" to show that time travel was impossible because we cannot accommodate it within our linguistic conventions. Donald Williams argued, "Time travel, *prima facie,* . . . is analyzable either as the banality that at each moment we occupy a different moment from the one we occupied before, or the contradiction that at each different moment we occupy a different moment from the one which we are then occupying—that five minutes from now, for example, I may be a hundred years from now."[9] Science fiction writers have simply ignored such criticism and have expanded our conceptual horizons by introducing new descriptions of the time traveller's experiences and explanations of causal processes at work in time travel stories.

The most rigorous and consistent work of this type has been written by Robert A. Heinlein in "By His Bootstraps" and "—All You Zombies." These stories are cited at the outset of a philosophical article recently written by Professor David Lewis of Princeton, which begins: "Time travel, I maintain, is possible. . . . I shall be concerned here with the sort of time travel which is recounted in science fiction."[10] Social philosophers can also learn a great deal from science fiction writers who earn their living by fleshing out the sketchy utopian blueprints of Plato, Marx, and assorted anarchists. Sometimes the resulting creations are favorable to the ideal, but authors like George Orwell, Aldous

Huxley, Ayn Rand, and Ira Levin have tried to show essential facts and human values that are overlooked or imperiled by the abstract theorists.

Persuasive science fiction can show the philosopher a new perspective on an old problem such as the nature of the mind. Roger Zelazny, in a beautifully written story, "For Breath I Tarry,"[11] describes the efforts of a machine named Frost to "become human." It is presupposed that Frost can simulate intelligent human activity such as speech and that it exemplifies the behavior characteristics of curiosity and desire. Zelazny provides an imaginative portrayal of what it would be like to be a robot trying to become human after all the real humans have perished from the face of the earth.

Frost is continually reminded by a mechanical companion Mordel that its efforts are fruitless because it can only mimic human behavior. For instance, it can imitate the behavior of a human artist but it does not have aesthetic experiences. Frost goes so far as to design "analogues of human sensory equipment" and contemplate scenery:

> "Now, direct my attention to an object or objects of beauty."
> "As I understand it, it is all around you here," said Mordel.
> The purring noise increased within Frost, followed by more clickings.
> "What do you see, hear, taste, smell?" asked Mordel.
> "Everything I did before," replied Frost, "but within a more limited range."
> "You do not perceive any beauty?"
> "Perhaps none remains after so long a time," said Frost.
> "It is not supposed to be the sort of thing which gets used up," said Mordel. . . . "Here comes a sunset. . . . Try that."
> Frost shifted his bulk so that his eyes faced the setting sun. He caused them to blink against the brightness.
> After it was finished, Mordel asked, "What was it like?"
> "Like a sunrise, in reverse."
> "Nothing special?"
> "No . . ."

Frost and his companion Mordel are more honest, we think, than contemporary behaviorist philosophers who have performed the sleight of hand of replacing consciousness with behavior in articulating a philosophical psychology. The machines recognize that what they are missing is the distinctively human mode of awareness. Mordel contends,

> "Regard this piece of ice, mighty Frost. You can tell me its composition, dimension, weight, temperature. A man could not look at it and do that. A man could make tools which would tell him these things, but he still would not *know* measurement as you know it. What he *would* know of it, though, is a thing that you *cannot* know."
> "What is that?"
> "That it is cold," said Mordel, and tossed it away.
> " 'Cold' is a relative term."
> "Yes. Relative to Man."

Mordel insists,

> ". . . There is no formula for a feeling. There is *no* conversion factor for an emotion."
> "There must be," said Frost. "If a thing exists, it is knowable."
> "You are speaking again of measurement. I am talking about a quality of experience. A machine is a Man turned inside-out, because it can describe all the details of a process, which a Man cannot, but it cannot experience the process itself, as a Man can."

The robot Mordel is making an interesting claim about the irreducibility of the phenomenon of consciousness. Like certain philosophers, Mordel suggests that certain facts about our consciousness are known by *introspection* and that these facts are not to be confused with physical facts that a machine can measure. Mordel suggests that one can have a complete description of the internal workings of an entity like man without comprehending the conscious experiences of that entity. Whether or not this line of reasoning can be sustained, it provides an interesting perspective on the nature of consciousness, one which has its counterpart in philosophical works such as Thomas Nagel's classic paper, "What Is It Like to Be a Bat?"[12]

We have argued that science fiction by its very nature serves the purposes of philosophy. This view is not universally held. An opposing conception of science fiction is vigorously argued by Isaac Asimov in the article, "When Aristotle Fails, Try Science Fiction." Asimov believes that science fiction is essentially wedded to the scientific method rather than to the philosophical enterprise. He denies that science fiction is concerned with the same perennial problems or "eternal verities" as traditional, mainstream literature.

> If we consider Literature (with a capital L) as a vehicle of ideas, we can only conclude that, by and large, the ideas with which it is concerned are the same ideas that Homer and Aeschylus struggled with. They are well worth discussing, I am sure; even fun. There is enough there to keep an infinite number of minds busy for an infinite amount of time, but they weren't settled and aren't settled.
>
> It is these "eternal verities" that are precisely what science fiction doesn't deal with. Science fiction deals with change. It deals with the possible advance in science and with the potential changes – even in those damned eternal verities – this may bring about in society.[13]

In the wake of scientific revolution and rapid technological change, our generation "can't take as its primary concern the age-old questions that have agitated all deep thinkers since civilization began." Asimov compares our culture to a rapidly accelerating automobile, its driver spending increasingly less time on "the eternal beauties of the scenery" and more on "the trivial obstacles in the road ahead." Asimov is critical of "new wave" critics like Kate Wilhelm who defend "purely literary science fiction."

Asimov's essay is polemical in tone and probably deliberately overstated for effect, but he is undoubtedly quite sincere in expressing his view of science fiction. Asimov is, quite properly, incensed by the "new wave" science fiction which in the late 1960s was parading eternal verities, mimicking stylistic experiments of the 1920s, and employing very, very sloppy science.

We are sympathetic with the view that a responsible science fiction author will be rigorous in projecting an alternative possibility. Nothing is more irritating than a time travel story rife with unnoticed and unresolved inconsistencies. But Asimov seems to be mistaken insofar as he considers the depiction of possible change as the purpose of science fiction. Its purpose is rather to provide the artistic means by which an author calls our attention to what is most essential or significant in human experience. This, of course, is the object of the eternal verities or perennial problems of philosophy.

The possible developments of the future hold our interest insofar as they relate to something which we now consider important. And we need to see clearly what is important if we are to survive and flourish in the future. To use Asimov's image of the accelerating automobile, a person without a philosophy of life is like a driver who is very attentive to particular obstacles on the road ahead but never consults a roadmap to figure out where he is going.

The point can be further illustrated by reference to the Asimov story with which we began. Why does "Reason" work as a story? Surely not because it is remotely probable that a computer on an interplanetary solar station will begin to spout Cartesian philosophy! We are impressed when science fiction writers make accurate predictions but we are not distressed when they are wide of the mark. The value of Asimov's story lies in its revelations about the essential nature of philosophical reasoning itself. Insofar as the plot seems possible, the story presents an effective critique of pure reason and an exercise in constructing ontological proofs of God's existence.

We have tried to present what we see as the value of science fiction for the philosophical enterprise. We won't go as far as Wilhelm, who suggests that science fiction writers have been the sole heirs of the great philosophical tradition, since modern philosophers after Russell have sold their birthright for a mess of linguistic pottage.[14] But we do maintain that philosophers ought to recognize, respect, and enjoy science fiction writers as auxiliaries in the joint pursuit of the truth.

2.

On Again, Off Again

LEE F. WERTH

Lee F. Werth has published a number of articles on a variety of topics, including the philosophy of science (with special regard to the concepts of space and time), metaphysics, and epistemology. He is also interested in paranormal phenomena, as is reflected by his article, "Normalizing the Paranormal," which appeared in the January 1978 issue of the American Philosophical Quarterly.

The following story merits our attention both as an excellent work of science fiction in its own right and as a careful attempt to illustrate the possibility of time travel.

Werth has taught at the University of Waterloo in Ontario, where he received his doctorate in philosophy, and at the Althouse College of Education at the University of Western Ontario. He is now an associate professor of philosophy at the Cleveland State University, where he has taught since 1972.

In keeping with the dictum that one should tell the truth as though it were fiction and fiction as though it were the truth, I am presenting this story. For several years now I have desired to convey the following account; prior to this I have mentioned it to no one. I welcome the present opportunity to unburden myself. God knows I need the catharsis and if I am right, no one will believe my account to be anything but fiction.

I thus regard myself for the moment as being rather fortunate—I have the opportunity to entertain others, that is, I can help relieve their tensions while I also relieve my own. Since human beings are the strange animals they are, it is indeed possible to entertain them by relaying to them the misfortunes of others of their kind. One wonders whether watching Hamlet is altogether different from gawking at a fatal traffic accident. This story too has its fatal accident, yet fatal in a most peculiar sense.

I am a philosophy professor in a midwestern state university. Does this seem a trite enough beginning? Good! I am doing very well at telling the truth as though it were fiction. The usual problems plagued my academic habitat, probably less so than at other places. The problems remain today and for the most part they are less likely to yield crisis than corrosion.

In any case, I was feeling somewhat corroded when a friend in the physics department called me and insisted that "we must talk immediately about a matter of extreme urgency requiring the greatest discretion."

My friend, whom I shall name in a moment, frequently talked in a manner that was virtually a parody of a pedant. He is to be forgiven, however, since English, or perhaps I should say Academese, is his sixth language. I wasn't at all surprised by his phraseology, but I was genuinely shocked by his anxiety.

Perhaps I will be taking the chance that my friend's identity will be revealed, but I am going to call him Professor Ho Hum. And why not? That's what the students call him, at least the less inspired ones who can understand his academic English even less than they can his mathematical models.

Since Ho was rather far from being his usual inscrutable self, it seemed wise to meet with him somewhere where he would not be seen by either my departmental colleagues or his.

Ho Hum is a calm, extremely self-disciplined and meticulous

scholar. He is that sort of self-effacing person who is so genuinely unaware of the magnitude of his own talents that he always seems slightly amazed when someone, a colleague perhaps, says something patently idiotic. Ho at such times looks for the hidden profundity of the remark, more often than not finds it, never realizing that the remark was as stupid as it *prima facie* seemed to be. He then goes off with the impression that his colleague is an amazing and subtle thinker whereas I go off realizing that Ho is a genius, a man who can find order in chaos. As might be imagined Ho was a great favorite with the faculty. Everyone, myself included, enjoyed hearing how interesting "their" ideas were. I was rather fond of Ho and was quite frankly rather shaken to find him so utterly shattered.

If anyone in the physics department other than Professor Ho Hum had told me the following series of events, I would have concluded that an elaborate practical joke was being played on me, no doubt because I sometimes claim to be a philosopher of science who allegedly knows a little about the nature of time. Moreover, I am certain that others will conclude from this story that I indeed was the butt of such a joke. Unfortunately, I had occasion to see the source of Dr. Hum's anguish.

I thought Ho called me not because of my professional specialty but simply because I was a philosopher and at the time he seemed in need of one. Hence I was all primed to tell him, gently of course, that though I might indeed be a comparatively effective *academic* philosopher, unlike Socrates, I was not in fact wiser than other men. However, I resolved to hear Ho Hum out, since it was the least I could do — and I suspected also the most I could do.

Ho and I met at a quiet and unfrequented spot in the library, the philosophy section. Ho asked me in an uncharacteristic manner (that is, leaving aside all pleasantries and abandoning all graciousness) whether I knew a certain member of the mathematics department. I acknowledged that I did. He asked how well I knew him. I replied that I knew him well enough to know that I did not wish to know him better, but that I needn't worry about that since he was on sabbatical leave.

Ho acknowledged that the scholar presently at issue was not the most loved of men. Though professionally quite competent (meaning only that his articles were first rate) he was by anyone's assessment of emotional maturity an adolescent. Even his youngest students made allowances for him. I did not know it then, but Ho was probably the only one on campus who was regarded as a friend by this particular person whom I shall call Dr. Frederick Hitzkopf. At this point I had best simply relate what Ho told me in the philosophy section of the library. It seems as though Ho had been both an intellectual companion and guru of a sort to Professor Hitzkopf. It was difficult for me to imagine Ho as a Zen master. He seemed interested only in physics, and whenever I tried to discuss Zen with him he always giggled. Though I was ready for a mantra, a koan, a parable, or a paradox, I was nonplussed by a giggle. In retrospect I see that a giggle was exactly the right thing for an academic philosopher. Ho was indeed a Zen master.

In any case, he and Hitzkopf had had a long-standing "family" relationship—Ho as the father, offering counsel in all matters requiring patience, prudence, and equanimity; Hitzkopf as the son, impetuous and impulsive, intolerant, but capable of doing the heavy lifting, that is, of constructing alternative mathematical models for Ho Hum's physical theories.

Hitzkopf would often come to Ho in despair about the state of twentieth-century living. According to Ho, Hitzkopf had a common enough dream. He wished to retreat to a log cabin, one to be built by his own hands, to raise his own food, make his own clothes, and act as his own government and society. I told Ho that I would be more than happy to help Hitzkopf reach his goal. I offered my double-edged ax to the cause.

But poor Ho was receptive neither to humor nor irony, and simply went on to say that Hitzkopf insisted that he begin naked and without tools. It was Hitzkopf's intention to begin in the Stone Age and work his way back into the twentieth century. Naturally I pointed out that Hitzkopf already lived in the twentieth century, so what possible purpose could be served by his rearriving at it. Ho said that Hitzkopf desired the struggle. I pointed out that there was struggle enough just trying to combat worldwide starvation, war and illiteracy. Ho quite agreed, but also knew that such an argument would not convince Hitzkopf.

I gathered that if Hitzkopf was to gain enlightenment he must enlighten himself. Arguments served no purpose; even if intellectual agreement were reached, on an emotional level Hitzkopf wanted an out. I asked Ho if perhaps Fred Hitzkopf was an escapist. Was simple escapism being clothed in the rhetoric of struggle? He seemed to think so.

"Why didn't Hitzkopf go off into the woods and build his cabin?" I asked. "There's nothing quite like implementation to reveal the lie of romanticism and unwarranted sentimentality."

Ho's response surprised me. "Cynicism too is a form of escapism. All things considered I prefer the romantic to the cynic. There is art in the former and the possibility of love."

"Genuine love?" I asked. The conversation was casting a dreamlike aura over the whole proceeding. "I have known too many romantics who write their books on love, creating their art while their children cry for lack of any genuine affection."

"An interest in love is at least, how do you say it?, a foot in the door. Genuine love may at last enter," rejoined Ho.

I was becoming confused and impatient, particularly since I still didn't know the reason for our library meeting. "Well then, why doesn't the romantic Dr. Hitzkopf simply go off into the woods and build his cabin?"

"It can't be done today," said Ho. "We used to discuss Fred's intentions. He would tell me about zoning laws, national forests, and all manner of restrictions which would render implementation impossible. At first I thought he was . . . hedging. Is that the word? I finally came to understand the nature of the difficulty. If indeed an appropriate place could be found, a place where it would be legal to build a log cabin, it could not satisfy Fred's yearning."

"Of course not," I said. "His expectations are childish and unrealistic. If a hobby or an extended isolation would improve his temperament, that's one thing. But if he literally wishes to escape the twentieth century he'll never succeed. Every condensation trail left by a stratocruiser will remind him of the reality he would escape. It's also quite likely that whatever undisturbed little paradise he finds will eventually be overrun with geologists, recreational vehicles, bulldozers, and finally cement."

"He agrees with you," said Ho. "He understands that the whole enterprise would degenerate into playacting if even the smallest sign of the times, is that the expression?, could be seen."

"If you agree not only that Hitzkopf is an escapist but also that there is no place on Earth where he might recapitulate humanity's struggle from stones to stars, then I am afraid I see the point of this conversation even less than my reason for being here."

I was furious with myself as soon as I said this. Ho was upset about something and certainly did not deserve abuse from me. Ho obviously felt that he had to lead up to whatever was bothering him and I had forced the issue. I expected he would reveal that Hitzkopf had threatened to actuate a nuclear device, or poison the city's water supply, or some such thing. When Ho did respond I didn't understand him at first. And when I did I was sure that I did not.

"As I have said, Fred agrees with you. Presently, there's no place left on Earth for his experiment, which is why he had to go off into the past."

"Where did he go? Some Third World country?"

"No, he's right here, or rather, he's in my lab."

"I don't understand. He's returned already?"

"No, he hasn't, and he's three hours overdue already."

"Look Ho, I'm sorry, I must have missed something. If Hitzkopf is in your lab, then how can he be overdue? Was he supposed to meet us here, or were you supposed to meet him?"

"Yes, he was supposed to meet me in the lab three hours ago."

"Oh, I see. He's simply late. He was supposed to be in your lab before now. Frankly, I've never known him to be on time."

"No, he was there all right, he just hadn't come back when he was supposed to. I checked him and he wasn't back yet. He's still gone. I don't understand what happened. I don't know what to do. You know about time. Can you help?"

"I'll be glad to help you any way I can, Ho, but I still don't know what you're saying. You said you checked him and he wasn't back yet. You mean you checked before to see if he was there? What does time have to do with it?" My mind was racing. Did Ho think I was a psychologist who could help Hitzkopf become punctual by using behavior modification techniques on him? Was Ho having a nervous break-down? "Ho, my field is philosophy, not . . ."

"Of course. You have written about the nature of time. That's why you may be able to help me."

"To do what, Ho?"

"To find out why Fred hasn't returned to the present."

I finally understood what Ho Hum was saying. Worse yet, I believed him. There was obviously no joke involved and Ho was too reliable a scholar and experimentalist to have misunderstood the situation. Hitzkopf was apparently lost in past time.

Ho was right about one thing: I did know enough about time to know that time travel was not *a priori* impossible as many believe. But my mind recoiled just then. I had irrelevant, defensive thoughts which protected me from having to think about the hideous ramifications of what I had just learned. I did not think about time. Instead I thought how curious it was that Ho's English became less pretentious and more conversational when he was upset, whereas my own became more pedantic. Finally I was able to address the issue.

"Perhaps Hitzkopf decided to remain in past time. Maybe he's built his cabin and is quite satisfied. Maybe he had an accident and died. Perhaps . . ."

"You don't understand. His body is in my lab at the moment. But, of course, it's totally devoid of consciousness."

"Of course," I said. Of course? If I could help Ho it would be accidentally. I might inadvertently say something from which he would derive the solution to Hitzkopf's temporally wayward consciousness. God knows I didn't think I could help him any other way.

"Let me give you an analogy."

"By all means, Ho."

"Fred could no more choose to remain in the past than could an airplane pilot choose to remain in the air when his plane has run out of fuel."

I thought of sailplanes, soaring, thermals and the like, but wisely decided not to push Ho's analogy to the breaking point. "Ho, could you explain what the analogue of fuel is in the present case?"

"Fuel, what fuel?"

"The airplane stays up when it has fuel. What keeps Hitzkopf in past time?"

"Oh, the airplane analogy. There is no fuel as such. Fred's consciousness has simply been rerouted through what you would call spacetime. Given the route he selected he can't possibly stay away this long. Let me try another analogy. If a specific movie were shown, and ignoring the possibility of broken film, power failure, projector difficulties, etcetera, the movie would end at a predictable time, assuming you knew the projection speed and film length."

"Ho, I know nothing about all this, but maybe you shouldn't *ignore* this and *assume* that . . . Maybe . . ."

"No, my analogy misled you again. Let me explain this mathematically . . ."

I knew it would come to this. Nevertheless, I let him go ahead, since perhaps he would see the source of the problem if he went through the math again. On the other hand, I wondered whether Ho's devising analogies for me could consequently suggest a solution. One learns much by teaching others.

Then a perverse thought entered my mind: I wanted to see Hitzkopf, or rather, his body. Would he or it be staring into space? Would he look like a yogin sitting in lotus position? Perhaps he would appear catatonic. How had Ho been keeping Hitzkopf's body alive? What would its brain waves be like?

My thoughts rebounded from Hitzkopf's body to Hitzkopf. How can you build a log cabin when your body is stuck in someone's laboratory? Even if Hitzkopf could return to past time ("return" is hardly the correct word), what possible good could it do him? He would know that it was playacting on the stage of lost time. Of course no one in the past would know, nor could he tell anyone, for fear of being declared a warlock or some such thing.

I began to see the strange psychological logic underlying this mad scenario. Is it playacting if your play is reality to your audience? If one's reality becomes a half-remembered dream gradually obscured by daily events, then one's "reality" becomes the eighteenth century, or whatever, and the dream (a nightmare of impotence, alienation, and impending nuclear war, and if not war then demographic disaster bringing forth starvation, disease, and pollution) is a dream which at last gradually fades away. Slowly one regains the sense of having control over one's life. Hitzkopf standing ax in hand in the "past" gradually reconstitutes his psyche until he is ready again for "today."

I guessed that this was Ho's plan for him. I also suspected that Ho knew that the good old days were good only in retrospect and that Hitzkopf would soon develop a nostalgia for contemporary living. He would "return" a changed and better man. One's compassion can only increase when one encounters the "grand old realities" of diseases and abominable working conditions which we today have abolished, even if comparatively. Hitzkopf would at last gain emotional maturity.

Even supposing that I understood the psychological dynamics behind Ho's enterprise, there remained the still larger task of understanding the psychophysical nature of a world which allowed for Hitzkopf's escape into the past. Based on physical theory, such a journey is simply *a priori* impossible. Ho refuted all such theories when he sent Hitzkopf "back." Counterinstances can do that; even philosophers have difficulty quarreling with a fact. Yet something had apparently gone wrong and Hitzkopf had not returned.

Despite my vagrant thoughts I had largely attended to Ho's mathematical explanation.

"If I understand you, Ho, the physical world, if considered by itself, is a static and unchanging four-dimensional block. You're saying that time is not truly a feature of this block-universe *per se*. On the contrary, temporal relations relate our *experiences* to one another; the physical world itself is nontemporal. Let me see if I've got this. Our consciousness, you say, intersects this four-dimensional block at different locations and in so doing generates a series of three-dimensional intersections which accounts for our normal experiences of a seemingly three-dimensional world. Am I right so far?"

"More or less. I don't think I would say that the physical world *is* a four-dimensional structure; I would be more inclined to say that one can construct a mathematical model of the physical world, representing it as a four-dimensional structure. That is, I would not presume to tell the world what it really is."

"O.K., Ho, I see what you mean, but in any case do I have the model, as you put it, correctly characterized?"

"I believe so."

"All right then. The problem is this: Hitzkopf's consciousness is intersecting or sort of slicing into regions of this four-dimensional block which are, how should I put it?, temporally distant from 'here,' and for some reason he can't intersect those regions which we are presently intersecting and he's stuck some*when* else. That's what I would have to say isn't it? 'Somewhen'?"

"No, you should stick with 'somewhere.' Fred is some*where* else with respect to those regions his consciousness is intersecting. We're here, he's elsewhere. It's because his consciousness intersects elsewhere that he experiences what would be the past from our standpoint or location.

"You understand what I mean? Temporal distinctions such as earlier-later and past-present-future relate only to our experiences. The four-dimensional structure is not as it is ordinarily thought, that is, a space-*time* structure. I suppose I would have to call it a space-*space* structure. Just as a Euclidean sphere is nontemporal as Plato construed it, likewise the four-dimensional block has regions which are in no way temporally related to one another. As elements which are experienced, or as successively different experiences, there is a sense in which we can speak of a physical time series, but the elements *per se* are no more to be understood as temporally related than are the sides of the Great Pyramid in Egypt. If you first see one side, later another, still later another side, et-cetera, it is not the sides of the Great Pyramid which are earlier or later than one another, it is your experiences of the respectively different sides which are so related."

"And Hitzkopf is stuck looking at side two while we are looking at side three," I interrupted.

Ho continued, "One, two—the number is arbitrary. One is no more earlier than two with respect to the four-dimensional structure than is the number one earlier than the number two with respect to the natural numbers."

"Wait a minute, I'm confused. Number two is the successor to number one. Don't we have serially ordered elements in the four-dimensional structure?"

"Of course, and not simply a one-dimensional series of elements. But please don't misunderstand me. A successor needn't be a *temporal* successor. The number mapping is arbitrary, that is, three, two, one, or one, two, three—it doesn't matter. There's no preferred 'direction.' Do you see what this implies?"

"No, I'm not sure that I do."

"Let me return to my film analogy, but only if you promise not to abuse it."

I was glad to see Ho becoming more his usual self. I was tempted to say that I would sooner abuse my children than an analogy, but fortunately I remembered the seriousness of the occasion. Though I genuinely believed Hitzkopf to be a prisoner of time, frankly, I found the whole thing "unbelievable." That is, the truth hadn't come home to me emotionally.

He elaborated upon his analogy. "One could project a reel of film backwards. It hardly matters to the film. It matters to us, of course, but with respect to the film it is arbitrary. It depends on how the reel is wound, the rotation of the drive sprocket in the projector, but not upon the photographs which comprise the frames which constitute the reel of film. Think of these frames as being the elements of the four-dimensional structure. Consider the direction of projection as being the 'direction' of time, or as Eddington might say, time's 'arrow.' The projector is consciousness intersecting successively different elements (frames) of the four-dimensional structure. From the film analogy it becomes apparent that there is no preferred direction of time which is based upon the four-dimensional structure as such. The frames of the movie reel simply coexist as frames. Their serial ordering becomes a temporal series for us only upon projection. Only then are we conscious of action and process and time's 'arrow.' From the analogy you can see that both time and the direction of time are the result of consciousness projecting a series of elements from the four-dimensional structure. I could further elaborate upon the analogy but perhaps I should ask if you have any questions."

Again I wanted to push the analogy and ask Ho whether Hitzkopf's metaphorical projector had broken down in some way. Instead I asked, "Ho, what are the consequences of having a four-dimensional structure rather than a one-dimensional one? The film analogy would seem to constrain Hitzkopf. If Hitzkopf's 'return' to an earlier portion

.of the movie strictly follows the logic of the film strip analogy, then his time trip is as predetermined as a movie, even if shown backwards. Where is there room for freedom of choice? How can he have free will?"

"The way you put the question shows me that you can also answer it. Obviously the analogy breaks down at this point, unless we want to invent a new kind of film strip which looks a bit like a tree, not to mention a new sort of projector which has gates in it, or for that matter, a new moviegoer who presses buttons to determine which film strip branches are to be projected. Fred isn't locked into a one-dimensional series. Simply because the history of our *experiences* can be ordered in terms of a one-dimensional temporal series it does not necessarily follow that the elements we experience are themselves so ordered. Why take a logical property of human experience ordering and consider it also to be a property of the physical world? It's rather arrogant of us, don't you think? Fred's freedom is simply the freedom to work out alternative projection routes through the four-dimensional structure. He can project various series of three-dimensional intersections onto the 'screen' of his awareness more or less as he pleases. He did not wish to, of course, but he might have projected so as to see the world as a three-dimensional movie being run backwards, or sideways, or whatever. It seems paradoxical, but Fred, or anyone else, has virtually all the freedom they could want even though the physical world as a four-dimensional structure is itself absolutely timeless and immutable."

I was feeling queasy. I looked around the library and I did not feel the freedom—I felt locked into time, a prisoner of my body. I stared at my hands. It was not a movie, damn it, not even a metaphorical movie. I flirted with the idea that I was being had, that Ho was in fact putting me on. Why not? Wasn't he allowed to have a sense of humor? If I believed him then I was simply a credulous sort of fool. I began to embrace the idea and almost felt relieved that I could dismiss the idea of time travel as being at best a sort of conceptual toy, at worst paradoxical. I gave Ho a look of incredulity. Ho misunderstood it and in so doing made me again a believer.

"You don't believe it's possible to work out the route. I understand. I said as much to Fred. The theoretical possibility was there. I could see that. But the practical problems seemed staggering. How would he alter his temporal perspective so as to project a different region of the four-dimensional structure onto his consciousness? Assuming he succeeded in that, how would he remember who he is, or was or will again be? What body, if any, would he experience as being his body? If he 'returns' and begins again to project this region, our present region, or the region which we regard as present, our here-and-now, will he remember where he was? He shrugged these questions off and said that is what mathematicians are for. They are rather used to trafficking with infinity; indeed they quite enjoy it.

"He reminded me that even without a time 'machine' there are people who remember their earlier incarnations and still others who know the future. Surely with the proper mathematical model at one's disposal anyone can have such seemingly occult experiences. Just as some persons know when and where to look for a solar eclipse simply because they have a theory to work with, these persons seeming magicians to the primitive tribesman who can only see a solar eclipse by 'chance', in similar fashion Fred could know how to go about experiencing the past and future through the employment of the proper model. To date people have had such seemingly occult experiences merely by chance and dumb luck. He argued that magic is reducible to mathematics."

I did not expect this new turn in our conversation. I had quite forgotten that Ho, being an Easterner, was quite naturally familiar with Eastern religion. Somehow, though, I hadn't anticipated being obliged to accept reincarnation along with time travel. My queasiness was accentuated; I felt increasingly ill.

"Ho, if you're putting me on I implore you to tell me so now . . . I . . . I feel sick. This is too much to take all at once."

"Putting you on what? Oh! I know what you mean. No, I wish it were all a joke though I am not so unkind as to play such a joke on anyone. I can see that you don't really consider it a joke and that you do understand the problem. That is why I came to you. Others might believe that I was seriously ill, or psychotic. It is to your credit that you now feel sick. Should I leave you alone for a few minutes?"

"No. Let's get on with it. Am I now to consider reincarnation a fact along with time travel?"

"I have lived with Westerners long enough to understand how difficult it is for them to think of themselves as being anything else but their bodies. Of course, Christians and others speak of the soul or the spirit but they do so more by convention than conviction. One rarely encounters a well-educated Westerner who quite openly and sincerely speaks of the soul, and were one to find such a man he still would not speak of it knowledgeably. Many who fancy themselves intellectuals are happy enough believing that they *are* bodies, that they are biological machines, and that the most profound rapture is nothing but a brain process."

Here I was on guard. Frankly I have known too many physicists who advance their personal religious views behind the protective shield of scientific reputations. Einstein was not exempt from this and I should expect no better from Ho. Perhaps, too, it was professional jealousy—no one listens to an academic philosopher when he speaks about religion, yet everyone listens to the physicist. It was clear, however, that I had to question Ho on the subject.

"Ho, do you mean to say that you know the nature of the soul and that it's relevant to Hitzkopf's disappearance?"

"The world 'soul' seems to cause you intellectual discomfort. No matter. Let me use the word 'consciousness'—or perhaps 'awareness'. You are no doubt familiar with the tradition of Cartesian dualism. Western mind-body dualisms all involve an error which obscures the nature of the soul."

"Ho, you said you . . ."

"I'm sorry. Western dualisms distort the nature of consciousness by dividing the human being into two sorts of event series, the series of thoughts or mental events and the series of bodily movements or physical events. Much of your philosophical tradition seems to be not unlike those governments which are run by two major parties—sometimes the Mentalists dominate, sometimes the Physicalists. On occasion there is even a coalition government."

"You're speaking of Idealism and Materialism. Mentalists are Idealists?"

"Yes. Now, if I understand your tradition it seems that either the physical is to be reduced to the mental, or conversely, or else some unhappy compromise is reached in which the reduction is avoided but not with any appreciable gain in clarity. For example, if mind and body are held to be irreducible to one another, and if mental events and physical events are said to be simply two aspects of the same process, two sides of the same coin, what do we gain in understanding the relation between mind and body? So long as we begin by stating the relation between mind and body as one which involves *prima facie* two sorts of events, mental and physical, the problem is insoluble.

"Stating it in terms of two sorts of stuff or substance, spirit and matter, which have the attributes of thought and extension, or Descartes' solution, surprisingly is more helpful than stating the relation in terms of two event types, mental and physical. Descartes was closer to the truth than philosophers today."

"Ho, you are talking about mind and body. I thought you were going to explain the nature of consciousness. The mind-body relation is different than the consciousness-object of consciousness relation, isn't it?"

"Decartes was aware of his consciousness. He was aware of its activity. He also intuited that this activity *qua* activity was somehow more fundamental than the objects of consciousness. The activity of consciousness was self-evident. Hence he could say, 'Ego cogito; ego sum.' The reality of the objects of consciousness as being anything else than experiences was, however, dubitable. Yet he went about trying to prove that his hands really existed, his eyes, and whatnot—that it was not merely a dream."

"Ho, please just tell me your position, then we can go back and look at the arguments supporting it."

"What an extremely odd thing for a professional philosopher to say. All right, I hadn't planned on giving a lecture on Descartes' philosophy. I just wanted to find someone with whom you're already familiar in order to help me make my point about consciousness."

"Which is?"

"Which is that Descartes was correct when he claimed that there is an indestructable acting subject, the soul or consciousness. He was incorrect when he claimed that his hands, eyes, etcetera, really existed. These were simply *experiences* which resulted when his consciousness intersected the four-dimensional structure, the block universe, so as to produce a series of experiences of a three-dimensional physical world in process. But the physical world is not *per se* a world in process—it is static and immutable. There is no true series of physical *events*. The only process, the sole activity, is the process of consciousness intersecting the block universe and projecting (metaphorically) three-dimensional intersections on the 'screen' of consciousness. This one and fundamental process does not require time. It doesn't 'take' time. On the contrary, it generates time. Time is mind-dependent, not a feature of the block universe."

"Ho, I believe I follow this, but what does it have to do with reincarnation?"

"Why don't you see? Consciousness could intersect the block structure in a manner which would produce the experience of having a different body than your present one. It can be compared to a moviegoer watching a double feature. Movie reels coexist in the film library. They can be selected and projected by choice. Fred chose to watch a different movie."

"We are entirely passive then, like moviegoers?"

"You promised not to abuse the analogy. If a moviegoer was also the character on the screen, and if he could feel and touch as well as see and hear—well, you begin to get the idea—he would be actively living the life of the character on the screen and he would not fancy himself passive. Yet the only activity is that of consciousness slicing away at the block universe so as to produce the series of three-dimensional intersections."

"Fine, but that hardly explains why we intersect and experience what we do when we do in the way we do. It may be that other consciousnesses are declaring 1777 to be their present, and if so, why should it be so?"

"It depends upon the nature of their ignorance. All 'places' and all 'times' are in principle available for projection. You could project every frame of every movie at 'once,' an ultimate superimposition of absolutely every element of the four-dimensional block structure, a structure which is in reality, I suspect, of infinite dimensionality. Or you could edit the 'film' and project much less. You've seen those movies of flowers growing, haven't you? By intersecting the block universe at loci further apart from one another than we ordinarily do, you could see or be aware of the continents drifting about on the planet's surface. Or you could see a mountain range cresting and tumbling as you would ordinarily watch the waves upon the sea."

"Would I experience myself as having a human body?"

"That you even ask such a question shows you know the answer. Perhaps you would find yourself a stone among a society of stones. Your temporal perspective would be distended over eons. Our ordinary minute would have no meaning to you. Moreover, consciousness could just as easily intersect elements of the four-dimensional block which are closer to one another than are those which we *qua* human beings customarily intersect; a running man would appear to such a consciousness as immobile as a stone appears to be to us. It's all a function of ignorance."

"Ignorance? I don't understand."

"Your consciousness could in principle intersect and project every element of the block universe at 'every time.' Such is the nature of *satori*. (*Satori* is a word Westerners seem to know though I have never known just why.)"

"Wait a minute Ho, if my consciousness projected every element at every time, my experience would not be a series of events. It would be, to use the film analogy again, like watching a slide rather than a movie. Nothing would move nor change. It would be as though I had superimposed every frame of an ordinary movie and then projected the superimposition for two hours—a very dull movie indeed."

"Don't abuse the analogy. In one sense yes, a dull movie—no change would be apparent, there would be no events as such. Yet in another sense *everything* would be "happening" at every "time." All the information would be available on tap. It would be up to you, your consciousness, to draw particular information bits out of the total superimposition and to attend to these bits successively, that is, to attend to different information bits at different times. Then you would experience a movie, one of your own making. Of course, this would not entail that the superimposition itself had changed. Do you see what I am driving at?"

"I think so. I would find myself speaking in pseudo-Eastern paradoxes. I would say that everything is happening, therefore nothing is happening, and that if all things happen at all times then nothing happens at any time. There would be no change and thus no time. Yet we still retain logical consistency here on the interpretation you've given."

"Possibly. Certainly appearances of the physical world, what we would ordinarily call physical events, satisfy the demands of logical consistency. However, what I have called the superimposition of elements would be inconsistent as a superimposition. I suppose I could say that reality is inconsistent since a literal description of it would involve contradictions and that physical events are consistent since they are merely appearances. Yet I would rather say that reality is simply 'beyond' either consistency or inconsistency. Such distinctions seem to me relevant only to descriptions of events."

I was about to say something but Ho continued.

"Now let me ask you a question. Suppose you and I both penetrated the veil of ignorance and were aware of the superimposition *in toto* with no loss of information. And suppose we remained in this state. What does this say about us?"

"Did this happen to Hitzkopf?"

"No, of course not, least of all him."

"Least of all him? Oh, I see. He would have achieved enlightenment? Wait, I know what you're driving at. Personal identity is also merely appearance. Your consciousness is identical to mine if we 'both' are aware of the superimposition. There would be no basis for numerically distinguishing you from me."

"Yes, you seem to understand me, intellectually at least. It usually sounds like gibberish to a Westerner. Merely one more conceptual move is required of you. Perhaps I should say 'leap' rather than 'move.' This time I shall abuse the film analogy myself.

"If an individual person is defined on the basis of the unique series of experiences he has had, and if all individual consciousnesses, that is, persons, are in principle capable of experiencing 'everything,' the total superimposition, then individual persons can, in principle, coalesce into a 'single' world-consciousness. If I were to push the movie analogy I would say that this 'single' movie viewer is defined as the total awareness of the film, that is, of the superimposition in its entirety. The projector is that active or dynamic principle which is a necessary condition for the viewer's awareness. The screen is a passive principle, the metaphorical screen of consciousness, also a necessary condition for awareness. The superimposition film strip is the object of consciousness which *qua* object does not change.

"But it is far better here not to push the analogy in every aspect. A more useful movie metaphor would consist of a movie which projects itself onto itself and is aware of itself, that is, a self-projecting and self-aware superimposition."

"I see what you mean by 'conceptual leap.' I'm sorry, Ho, conceptual broad jumping is not my forte. Forget the movie metaphor. What are you saying?"

"Why, simply that consciousness ultimately has itself as its own object and that the distinction between consciousness and its object is a verbal distinction appropriate to appearances but not to reality as I have modeled it."

"Okay, Ho, let's suppose consciousness does have itself as its own object. What import does this have to Hitzkopf's disappearance?"

"Fred Hitzkopf was too much the patron of his own ego to make any progress through the usual methods of meditation. He strived to achieve *satori* as one might strive to be a millionaire. Naturally, it was self-defeating. We talked at great length about it. Fred was an artist at rationalization. At every turn his intellect thwarted any attempt at emotional development. I realized that I would have to let his intellect trap itself if he was to make any progress at all. As soon as he understood the implications of the four-dimensional block universe structure he became obsessed with the idea of returning to the past. I tried to guide him to the realization that it was the spaceless, timeless superimposition in its entirety which he was to contemplate, not some three-dimensional intersection series of it, not simply some other place or time.

"But it was no use. He was like a child with a new toy and could think of nothing else but 'going into the past,' or projecting that series which would provide him the environment he desired for his log cabin. By helping him achieve his escapist dream I thought he would learn the bitter fruits of his folly. He was utterly incapable of the most elemen-

tary form of meditation. His mind was always in a state of seething turbulence. There seemed nothing else to do but to alter his awareness by
altering his temporal perspective."

"And that is your time machine—a device for altering temporal perspective? Look, Ho, if you can alter temporal perspective with a machine, and if Hitzkopf can work out the mathematics so as to locate his
consciousness wherever and whenever he pleases, why not simply adjust your temporal perspective alterator, or whatever you call it, to
produce instant *satori*? Why bother with log cabins? Wouldn't
Hitzkopf let you do it?"

"You don't understand. Fred, as I have already said, craved nothing
so much as a *satori* experience. That was exactly his problem. A machine, even a time machine, can't instantly grant emotional maturity.
One must provide that for oneself. The most I could do was to provide
him with the appropriate learning experiences.

"If I had adjusted the machine so as to enable him to experience 'everything,' the total superimposition, to experience all elements of an
unchanging four-dimensional block in one act of awareness, it could
only have driven him mad. Consider the nature of such an experience:
There would be no objects as we have come to know them, no hands,
no eyes, no rooms nor people in them—only 'blackness,' a void, an
abyss. An unchanging awareness would be without memory, without
anticipation, without ego, a total annihilation of anything familiar.
Only an overwhelming horror would remain, and a craving for a
world, an identity, a body, a place and time—a striving for selfhood.
Yet this craving could be neither conceptualized nor articulated. There
would only be the awareness of falling, of an infinite loneliness, of an
empty anguish with neither form nor content. Nothingness."

An idea occurred to me. (Actually, many ideas occurred to me, most
of which I made every effort to suppress at the time, relating to what I
had read and heard of concerning 'escaping the wheel of Karma' and
the like. Fragments of Fichte flirted with Herman Weyl's metaphor of
consciousness 'crawling up world-lines,' bits of Buddhist moralizing
joined in to contribute an erratic counterpoint, but one idea dominated
over all others.)

"You tried it, didn't you Ho? You tried to have instant *satori*? You've
experienced this horror, haven't you?"

"It was clear to me that Fred was not ready for it, nor was I, I discovered. Such light is only for saints. Perhaps your Socrates could bear it but I must remain in the comfort of the cave.

"In any case I saw no harm in sending Fred into the past. Since the physical world as a four-dimensional structure is itself unalterable I had no worries concerning Fred being hurt or killed. If his consciousness intersected and projected a series of elements two hundred 'years' distant from the region he would normally project, this would not change the nature of the projected elements. And, if he should experience having another body, that would not change the one in my laboratory. The laboratory body now exists as a datum for our consciousness but not his, unless he's just 'returned.' I don't mean to imply that Fred's journey is, how do you say it?, 'no big thing.' However, the time paradoxes dearly beloved by science fiction writers do not arise, at least not in the usual way."

"Suppose Hitzkopf kills his father while his father is a boy of eight."

"Fred's father did not die at the age of eight, as Fred's body in my laboratory clearly demonstrates. There is at least one branch of the four-dimensional structure which includes Fred's father as a four-dimensional region and also Fred. I should also add that both Fred's and his father's body considered as four-dimensional regions are themselves branched. Were this not the case our lives would be fatalistic, our consciousnesses would be locked into projecting along a nonforking lifeline of our four-dimensional block bodies. However, the fact is that each fork or branching point provides consciousness with a choice situation. Hence free will is no illusion."

"Wait a minute, Ho. Couldn't there be a branch of Hitzkopf's father's block body which abruptly terminates, this short branch entailing a short life for his father were his father's consciousness to have chosen it rather than some other branch? Couldn't this short branch exist because Hitzkopf has chosen to meet his eight-year-old 'father' and to kill him?"

"Since Fred's body is in my lab, there is obviously no projection route in which Fred's consciousness could become incarnated as his eight-year-old 'father's' murderer."

"Ho, have you considered that Hitzkopf's consciousness might itself also branch, in which case he might have murdered his eight-year-old 'father' on one branch but allowed him to live on another, thus enabling this boy to become a man and hence Hitzkopf's father?"

"We thought of that, but again there would be no problem. Fred's consciousness would be able to return to my lab since the appropriate branch would be there. I must admit, though, that such things worried me, but Fred considered it all rather elementary."

"Even if Hitzkopf is able to project what for us would be the past, and even if 1777, or whatever, is the present from his temporal perspective, how would he remember who he is? How would he know that he is, was, will be, Fred Hitzkopf?"

"This was the first question I asked him. He pointed out that his consciousness would be 'looping back' through the four-dimensional structure rather than projecting 'ahead.' Forgive me now if I speak of future incarnations but it helps to answer your question. Your future bodies exist as elements in the four-dimensional branching structure. Indeed which of these bodies becomes experienced or projected as yours depends upon the choices you make now. Yet any of the possible bodies which your consciousness might subsequently project have not yet been projected. Of course, with the temporal perspective alternating device which Fred and I invented it is possible to send your consciousness ahead."

"Of course." I barely understood what Ho meant. As usual Ho's use of "of course" seemed most inappropriate.

"Ho, let me anticipate your answer: You're saying that a physical element once experienced by consciousness can be remembered, but that a possible future incarnation which has not yet been experienced as a three-dimensional physical process series cannot be remembered. Since Hitzkopf's consciousness has projected the body in your laboratory he is able to 'loop back' without loss of memory. If you're correct, then the past is relative to individual projection routes. There would be a separate temporal ordering of events for each individual consciousness."

"In principle, yes. But without the temporal perspective alterator, or in rare cases, chance, it is unlikely for your temporal perspective, for example, to become out of phase with mine. Hence we share our worlds, if I may put it that way."

"Ho, how was Hitzkopf able to work out the branching points? How could he plot his course through a branching four-dimensional structure?"

"This was the second question I put to him. We discussed the quantum mechanical problems. I argued that the probabilities became incalculable once randomness was thrown into the projection route problem. I said that he couldn't know anything about his intended route since the elements projected as a three-dimensional physical process series were indeterministic, at least on a quantum level. He countered by arguing that the macro-states were sufficiently calculable and it was the macro-states that his consciousness projected, not the indeterministic micro-state series. He said lightning would always bring forth thunder be it past, present, or future, and the hell with quantum mechanics. He said he could see lightning, not electrons."

"His philosophy of science seems a bit simplistic, or don't you think so, Ho?"

"At the time he seemed so confident, so hopeful, I somehow believed he could do it. I believed he could work out the route."

"Do you mean you've never seen his calculations?"

"He's not one for making notes and those he makes are all but illegible. I didn't want to pry into his private files. I couldn't bring myself to do it."

"Ho, Hitzkopf's life is at stake, his psychic life anyhow. 'Psychic' is not quite the word I want. You know what I mean."

"I wouldn't be here if I didn't."

"Let's look at his notes."

We returned to Ho's laboratory where Fred Hitzkopf's notes were locked in a file cabinet. I suspected that Ho's reservations weren't based upon considerations of Hitzkopf's privacy alone. Ho was afraid that he would discover something for which he would feel responsible. Knowing that, I wanted to be gentle with him. It seemed to me that whatever had happened to Hitzkopf, he had damned well asked for it.

Ho finally found Hitzkopf's calculations and studied them, looking rather puzzled.

"What's the matter Ho? Can't you read them?"

"No, I can read them all right. I don't understand them. From what I can tell Fred had the temporal perspective alterator set up to oscillate. He couldn't make such a simple mistake by accident."

"What do you mean, Ho, oscillate?"

"The way he had himself routed would be as though a movie would run a few frames backwards then forwards then backwards. Oh my God, how horrible! He's locked into a perpetual oscillation! His consciousness has become a pendulum. He's turned on the temporal perspective alterator, his consciousness unwinds back to the moment before when the temporal perspective alterator was off, then projects forward to when it's turned on, then unwinds to when it was off again, then on again, off again, on again, off again . . . oh my God, what have I done?"

"Ho! Why don't you simply readjust the time machine? Can't you reset the temporal perspective alterator?"

"No, I can't reset it. Once Fred's temporal perspective has been altered there's no way I can reach him. His temporalizing of events is out of phase with ours. There's nothing we can do. Why would he set the alterator to oscillate his consciousness? I don't understand it."

Nor did I understand it, not at first. I thought of Fred Hitzkopf, or rather I thought of his consciousness, as a sort of psychic Sisyphus, a man who wanted an easier world in which to live, who "now" is perpetually oscillating, his consciousness grinding forward only to be tossed back again into the past, then forward again, while his body and the rest of us leave him behind. In a way he achieves immortality, but at the price of infinite redundancy. Even he did not deserve that. And if Ho is right, then we are all immortal in any case. I began feeling compassion for Hitzkopf until I realized it was Ho who needed help. But then I understood what really had happened.

"Ho, you've been had. Hitzkopf knew very well what he was doing. He committed suicide. Don't you see? He wanted out, but on your theory he was doomed to perpetual reincarnations. Remember you said how he was such a poor student of meditation, how his mind was always in a state of seething turbulence? What else did he have to anticipate but endless future eons of the same? How else could he have killed himself?"

"No, I don't see. To be forever projecting the same event over and over again, that would have to be worse than living endless sequences of futile lives. No, I don't see what he could hope to gain."

"It's really very simple. He turns the temporal perspective alterator on with the hope of freeing himself from the burden of this life or any other, whereupon his consciousness unwinds, projects backwards, forgets. He 'unremembers.' He anticipates nothing and remembers nothing until an instant earlier is reached by his consciousness, the instant in which the temporal perspective alterator is off, or the very instant prior to his turning it on. His consciousness reverses and again he 'journeys' hopefully, with the expectation of psychological oblivion, which he achieves when the machine is again turned on. Again his consciousness unwinds. He oscillates between hope and oblivion. Based on your theory, what other form of suicide is there?"

"Do you think that's what he did? Commit suicide?"

"I am certain of it, Ho. He could not have done it by mistake."

"What shall we do with his body?"

I shall not say what Ho and I did with Fred Hitzkopf's body. We did destroy the temporal perspective alterator.

In any event I feel much better for having told this story. I hold no illusions that it will be read as anything but fiction. It hardly matters to me. I'm not sure I really want people to believe it. Small minds live better in a small world. Yet the account as I have stated it is not fiction. It happened as I have said it happened. No matter. Never mind.

3.

Tips for Time Travel

MONTE COOK

Monte Cook received both his bachelor's and doctoral degrees in philosophy at the University of Iowa, and specializes in early modern philosophy and contemporary analytic philosophy, fields in which he has published a number of papers in professional journals.

An earlier version of this essay, which considers some of the ramifications of time travel, was presented at the Popular Culture Association Convention at Pittsburgh in April 1979, and at the meetings of the Science Fiction Research Association at South Lake Tahoe, California, in June 1979.

Cook has been at the University of Oklahoma since 1968 and is an associate professor of philosophy.

Travel through time is an odd business. By reflecting a little on its oddities, a whole host of helpful tips on time travel emerge, including information on getting yourself a time machine, on using it once you've got it, and on the dangers, real and imagined, of travelling through time.

I will mainly be concerned with travel to the past, where time travel is at its oddest. And, though much of what I say will apply to all forms of time travel, I will concentrate on travel by time machine rather than travel through time warps or time portals. In fact, I will concentrate even more narrowly on what I will call, somewhat inaccurately, "Wellsian time machines." These machines never "jump" through time and space without travelling through intermediate times and places. Just as a person driving a car from Pittsburgh to New York travels along a path and never just jumps from the one city to the other, when travelling by Wellsian time machine from Pittsburgh in 1979 to New York in 1879, a person moves along a path from 1979 Pittsburgh to 1879 New York and never just jumps from the one to the other. In fact, a Wellsian time machine travelling from 1979 Pittsburgh to 1879 New York will appear to be a more ordinary vehicle slowly travelling in the opposite direction—it will seem to start at New York in 1879 and take one hundred years to travel to Pittsburgh.

Since most discussions of time travel so far have appeared in works of science fiction, I will draw on science fiction to clarify my tips for time travel. No one has invented a time machine, and so far as I know no one is working on one. Time machines—at least time machines for travelling into the past—are widely held to be impossible to invent. But this doesn't stop writers of science fiction from using the notion of time travel, even when they think it impossible. Some writers, of course, simply use time travel as a device to develop a plot having nothing particularly to do with time travel itself; but some of them seek to explore consequences of the very notion of time travel.[1]

DON'T WORRY ABOUT CHANGING THE PAST—YOU CAN'T

The first important tip I have is in reaction to a large body of science fiction literature. Some of you may be worried about what may happen if, while travelling, you change something in the past. After all, science fiction abounds with stories in which a time traveller changes the past and returns to the present to find everything changed.

Perhaps the most famous example is Ray Bradbury's "A Sound of Thunder," in which a time traveller kills a butterfly in the past and radically alters the present to which he returns.[2] (Most of us have seen the

"Star Trek" episode in which Bones goes through a time portal and saves the life of a woman in the past, with the result that the Starship Enterprise doesn't exist – and presumably never did.) Some may take comfort in the argument that we too would have changed, so that we wouldn't notice changes that resulted from tampering with the past.[3] But most of us want to return to a world that is at least pretty much the same as we left it, and find especially worrisome the notion that changing the past might even undo our own existence.

Though science fiction writers worry about changing the past, they are really worrying about changing the past in ways that have far-reaching effects. The writers usually assume that time travel requires at least one change of the past: before the invention of time travel the past did not contain any time travellers; after its invention the past does. The problem – the big unknown – is discovering what changes in the past will significantly affect the present. Some science fiction writers try to allay our fears by appealing to mysterious forces that prevent our changing the past too much.[4] Some devise elaborate precautions to prevent any significant change of the past. Thus in "A Sound of Thunder" Bradbury imagines a dinosaur hunt in which hunters, wearing sterilized clothing and oxygen masks, stand on a sterilized path floating six inches above the earth. The hunters are allowed to shoot only animals about to die anyway and are required to remove their bullets from the dead animals. It seems that one has to be extremely careful about changing the past.

My first tip is: don't worry about changing the past – you can't. Not only can you not change the past in any significant way, you cannot change the past in *any* way. To see why you can't change the past, let's consider an attempt to change the past. Suppose that you travel to Ford's Theater in Washington, D.C., on the fifteenth of April in 1865 and attempt to prevent Lincoln's assassination. One possibility is that something will go wrong and you will simply fail. Another remote possibility is that you will succeed and that we've been wrong all this time in thinking that Lincoln was assassinated, that in fact Lincoln died of something else or didn't die in April of 1865 at all and there was some sort of coverup.

What isn't possible is that Lincoln was assassinated before your interference and wasn't assassinated after your interference. Nor is it possible that you didn't exist in 1865 before stepping into the time machine and flipping the switch and did exist in 1865 after stepping into the time machine and flipping the switch. It is not as if 1865 had come around twice—once without your being there to prevent the assassination and once with your being there—so that the past had changed. There is no 1865 the first time (before you visited it) and another 1865 the second time (after you visited it); there is just 1865, and either you existed in 1865 or you didn't.

Mistakenly comparing travel into the past with ordinary travel assumes that the past can be changed. In ordinary travel you can go to places you've never been to and do things that you've never done before. But in travel into the past you can only go to times that you've already existed and do things that you've already done—otherwise it wouldn't be travel into the past. You don't remember having done the things that you did at these times, but if they are in the past then you have already done them.

By 1978, before you step into the time machine, you've already made your 1865 attempt to prevent Lincoln's assassination. Unless you've read about it in historical accounts, however, you don't know about it because you have no memory of doing so or of even being alive in 1865.

The you of 1865, in contrast, has not yet stepped into the time machine, but "remembers" stepping into the time machine and flipping the switch 114 years before it actually happens.

And after your return to the present, you have left 1979 for 1865, attempted to prevent Lincoln's assassination, and returned to 1979, and you remember all this. But your memory upon return does not fit the actual sequence of events: You remember first getting into the time machine, then attempting to prevent Lincoln's assassination, and lastly returning to 1979. If you think that your memory fits the actual sequence of events then you will think that your attempt to prevent Lincoln's assassination took place after you got into the time machine. But the very fact that you travelled into the past requires that your attempt to prevent Lincoln's assassination take place *before* you get into the time machine.[5]

I have given this tip partly because I wanted to show the folly of the widespread uneasiness about time travel, and partly because I wanted to expose at the outset a common misconception about time travel that has often led to a denial of its very possibility. I said earlier that science fiction writers usually assume that time travel requires some change of the past. But if it does and if changing the past is impossible, then time travel must be impossible.

Fortunately, time travel requires only that one be able to *affect* the past. Your stepping into the time machine and flipping the switch in 1979 must have some effect on the past; it must cause you and the machine to have existed in 1865. It need not, however, change the past.[6]

(A word of warning: since time travellers do affect the past, you still need to be careful. The fourteenth century plague called the Black Death is fact; nothing you do can change it. But you don't want it to turn out that you *caused* the Black Death by some bit of carelessness. While you can't *prevent* the Black Death, you can *cause* it.[7])

GETTING YOURSELF A TIME MACHINE

Assuming that your worries about changing the past and about the very possibility of time travel have been allayed, no doubt you want to know how to go about getting yourself a time machine. If you are a scientific genius perhaps you can invent yourself one, though even then you should find my suggestions valuable. But most of us are not scientific geniuses, so we have to get our time machines in some other way.

My first tip here is a warning: never buy a true Wellsian time machine for travel into the past. Unlike the modified Wellsian machine that I described earlier, the true Wellsian time machine only travels through time, not through space. That means that when you flip the switch to travel to 1879, the machine with you in it must already have been there, right on that spot, for one hundred years. (H. G. Wells himself anticipated this, arguing that the time machine travelled so fast that one couldn't see it.[8] But while to someone inside the time machine it may seem like a ten-minute trip and things will seem to happen very quickly, to someone on the outside the time machine will not be moving at all.)

The real problem with the true Wellsian time machine, however, is not that it must already be there on its backward journey before it departs; you might in fact see a time machine on its backward journey. The real problem is that a true Wellsian time machine would run into itself. The time machine on its pastward journey just after you flip the switch and the time machine sitting there just before you flip the switch will run into each other—both must occupy the same place at the same time.

So stick to modified Wellsian time machines and non-Wellsian time machines. About getting yourself a non-Wellsian time machine I have nothing helpful to suggest. But I do have some suggestions about getting yourself a (modified) Wellsian time machine. My main tip is: look for a Wellsian time machine travelling into the past and model your machine after it. With luck (lots of luck), you'll find such a machine with you in it.

In fact, suppose that you are smart enough to build a Wellsian time machine. What do you do then? Step in and flip the switch? But you know that it won't work, otherwise there would be a duplicate of the machine nearby (with you in it) on its journey into the past. Since you have to find such a duplicate anyway, why not use it as a model for the machine that you build?

I'm afraid that I have to add three sour notes to my tip that you look for a Wellsian time machine travelling into the past and model your machine after it. The first is that, unfortunately, you can't just borrow the machine that you find. Stepping into a moving time machine is an extremely dangerous business, and I strongly advise against it. No matter how quickly one steps into the machine there will be times that some parts of one's body don't exist. One second after you begin to board the machine, for example, your right arm and right leg may no longer exist because they may be on their way into the past. (I must confess a worry here that I might prove to be like those who once argued that the human body couldn't survive speeds over fifty miles per hour.)

The second sour note is that there is no use in attempting to flag your (future) self down for a ride (or to get him [you] to explain the principles on which the time machine works)—he's not going your way. Your future is his past and your past is his future. Since he is travelling back through time, even if he sees you trying to stop him and stops, his stopping will occur *before* you try to stop him. There is no reason for you to try to stop him because if your trying to stop him were to be effective he would already have stopped.

The final and most distressing note is that the duplicate time machine is likely to be very well camouflaged (or perhaps in a very inaccessible place). If a time machine had been moving between Pittsburgh and New York for one hundred years, then surely someone would have seen it by now — *unless* it is very well camouflaged indeed.

Fortunately, if you do find a time machine with you in it, you'll know that your attempt to travel through time succeeded. While you are looking for your time machine on its pastward voyage, I suggest looking for our time machine on its return voyage (most of us, I assume, want not only to travel to the past, but also to return). If you cannot find the returning machine, then I have several suggestions.

Assuming that you have found a time machine with you in it on its pastward voyage, you know that sooner or later you are going to take a trip in the time machine. But since you have reason to believe that you will never return, you might consider putting off the trip as long as possible. And when you do seek to return to the present, I suggest that you a) camouflage the machine in a way that you never considered when you originally looked for it, and b) return to a place that you never checked when you originally looked for it.

I should mention that returning to the present is in at least one way more dangerous than travelling to the past — if someone finds your return machine and sets out to destroy it, he may succeed; if someone finds the machine heading for the past and sets out to destroy it, he will fail because the presence of the time machine when he finds it already shows that he will fail when he tries to destroy it. If he were to be successful in destroying it, it wouldn't have been there earlier for him to find.

PLAY THE ODDS

Suppose that you've got a time machine; now you want to know how to use it. My general rule for time travel is a rule that I have appealed to already: play the odds. I used this rule when I suggested that any Wellsian time machine that has travelled into the past must have been very well camouflaged (or in a very inaccessible place)—odds are that an uncamouflaged machine would have been spotted by now. The real reason for time travellers to take certain kinds of precautions is not for them to avoid changing the past; the real reason (ignoring obvious practical reasons regarding their safety and welfare) is for them to play the odds.

If you want to visit Socrates' trial, don't dress in twentieth-century clothes—the odds against someone's having been present at Socrates' trial dressed in twentieth-century clothes are astronomical. If you want to visit Socrates' trial, dress appropriately, speak the language, know the customs, and so forth. In this way you will be playing the best odds for your having been present at the trial.

Of course, if the records of the time that you want to visit tell of a bizarrely dressed, strange-tongued, odd-acting visitor, you need to take that into account. (If your visit to the past can explain something that has hitherto been inexplicable, so much the better.)

The trick is to get as much information as possible about the time and place that you want to visit (and your route if you have a Wellsian time machine) and then to plan your trip based on that information. Once you have the information, you can estimate the probability of various courses of action and pick the one that shows the best chance of success.

Since the application of the rule that you should play the odds is a bit difficult to understand, I will clarify with an example. Suppose that you would like to visit your past self. Don't pick a time that you distinctly remember having been alone to visit—your attempt to visit yourself will fail. Pick a propitious time for visiting yourself, a time at which the probability that you visited yourself is higher than usual. In particular, pick a time that lends itself to a ready explanation of why you don't remember such a visit: you don't remember visiting your past self because your past self was very young, was sleeping, or whatever. Or perhaps you distinctly remember being stared at from a distance by a vaguely familiar-looking person, but you didn't know that it was your future self.

If you want not only to visit but also to talk with your past self, the chances of success drop; but there are still things that you can do – I suggest disguising yourself, talking to yourself as a young child (were you known as a very imaginative child?), and keeping your conversation unmemorable. Of course, if you were once visited by a mysterious stranger, take that into account.

A FINAL WARNING

I've given you tips about how to get yourself a time machine and how to use it once you've got it, and I've told you not to worry about changing the past. The rest is up to you.

I would be seriously amiss, however, if I neglected to give you a final warning about Wellsian time machines. At least twice H. G. Wells has his Time Traveller escape danger by fleeing into the future – once to escape carniverous beings called "Morlocks" and once to escape a giant crablike creature. My final tip is a warning: never, never try to escape danger by using a Wellsian time machine to flee into the future. Fleeing into the future will not get you out of danger with a Wellsian time machine; since Wellsian machines don't jump from one time to another, it will keep you in danger. You might as well try to escape danger by taking a nap.

4.

Will a Rubber Ball Still Bounce?

JOSEPH C. PITT

Joseph C. Pitt is a colleague of mine at Virginia Polytechnic Institute and State University, specializing in the history and philosophy of science. He received his bachelor's degree from The College of William and Mary and completed his doctorate at the University of Western Ontario. He has since published a number of articles on the history and philosophy of science, as well as collaborating on the editing of three books: on Galileo, on Wilfrid Sellars, and on the philosophy of economics.

I invited Pitt to read an earlier draft of the following essay to the Popular Culture Association Convention in Pittsburgh in 1978. He argues that most of the accounts of "alternative universes" that we find in science fiction are either merely different from ours while obeying the same laws, and thus not providing "alternatives" in any interesting sense, or are simply incoherent.

A continuing theme in science fiction concerns the structure of the universe and the principles that govern it. But while this idea is enduring, its mode of expression has changed. In the good old days—what

Asimov euphemistically calls the "Golden Age"—a favorite device for expressing our assumptions about the nature of the fundamental principles of the universe was to emphasize the expansion capacity of our extended though basically standard technologies. A look at more recent work reveals, however, that the earlier emphasis on technology is being replaced by a variety of efforts designed to explore some of the underlying features of nature in nonstandard ways.[1]

What I would like to explore here is the extent to which these newer efforts can succeed. I don't think they can, and for specific philosophical reasons. These are many and varied, so for the sake of specificity I intend to narrow the range of the discussion by concentrating on only one issue—the way in which the concept of causation operates in our understanding of the world and its effect on writing science fiction.

First, a few preliminary comments. The heart of the matter is that science fiction writers have failed miserably to construct believable alternative realities by abandoning our familiar concept of billiard ball cause-and-effect relations. (What I have in mind here is exemplified by Delaney's *The Einstein Intersection;* more on this later.)

They fail for two reasons. First, our common sense conception of causation is so fundamental, so pivotal in our thinking, that to tamper with it in other than extraordinarily limited ways leads to conceptual chaos. Second, because causation is fundamental to our conception of the mechanics of physical reality (and hence its very nature), no viable *alternative* universe can be constructed without abandoning it. It follows that since no such alternative can be constructed and still be intelligible, such efforts ought to be abandoned.

So, while this is essentially an essay in metaphysics, it has prescriptive overtones. I am suggesting that since science fiction that tries to describe alternative worlds in believable ways is doomed to fail for philosophical reasons, we should concentrate on doing something else. Let us see if the case can be made.

First we need to take a closer look at the notion of alternative worlds. (I intend to use the locutions "alternative world," "alternative universe," and "alternative reality" interchangeably, since nothing important here turns on it.) The kind of world represented in *Dune* is not what concerns me.[2] There we find an orderly environment—sparse, but operating according to rigid rules, all of which make perfectly good sense in terms of our own experiential base. Even the states of drug-induced foreknowledge are acceptable. Our acceptance of these situations is based, moreover, on just the same assumptions that allow us to accept our own experiences of *déjà vu* without going insane; in these cases we admit that something out of the ordinary has happened, but that sooner or later it will be explained by some scientific theory.

This is crucial in those fictional worlds where there are only a few "abnormal" phenomena thrown in, often just for appearance; the difference is smoothed over by our assumption that the causes behind such things are *in principle* knowable. It just might be that our heroes have not had the occasion to figure out what is happening, or more often that both reader and author acknowledge that these stray bits are merely color and not in any way essential to the story. In this latter situation, the assumption that the principles behind the phenomena are discoverable doesn't even enter in—we simply ignore the funny business and get on with the tale.

But in some cases we tacitly assume some explanatory device in the form of a scientific theory—a reductionistic principle seems implicit. It goes something like this: science will produce an explanation and we will be able to understand it because whatever science produces can be explained in ordinary terms. Such a principle is in evidence in much of science fiction. It's a pity it is false! Neither the potential of science to produce explanations for phenomena nor the accessibility of scientific explanation to common understanding is obvious. In fact, if we look at the history of science just the opposite seems the case. Science often fails to explain phenomena and when it does succeed, its explanations are not easily understood. But regardless of the ultimate status of the principle, that it is often invoked and, furthermore, that it is deemed acceptable seems to be the case.

There is a second type of situation in which the notion of an alternative world is not bothersome. This is exemplified by Stephen Donaldson in that fabulous scenario he creates in his Thomas Covenant series.[3] Granted, the rules are different in both the mode of the story and on the world in question. But whatever the specific causes, the kind of regularities employed in the story and the systematic reliance on

known causal principles are similar enough to our basic laws of cause
and effect for us to accept them. We are thereby in a position to accept
the scope of the action without having to know the particular manner
in which some of the processes essential to that world operate. This is
the same kind of thing that happens in *The Lord of the Rings*.[4]

No, the situation I have in mind is best exemplified by Silverberg's
"In the Jaws of Entropy"[5] and Delaney's *The Einstein Intersection*.[6] Let us
consider each of these briefly.

One of the most interesting features of Silverberg's piece is that he is
straightforward about what it is that he wants his hero to do.

> Won't you ever come to see that causality is merely an illusion, Skein?
> The notion that there's a consecutive series of events is nothing but a
> fraud. We impose form on our lives, we talk of time's arrow, we say
> that there's a flow from A through G and Q to Z, we make believe ev-
> erything is nicely linear. But it isn't, Skein. It isn't. (Silverberg, p.498)

Causal order is supposed to be illusory. Silverberg's aim is to get his
protagonist to recognize this and take command of the nonprocess
which is his life. He is to master the illusion of order and bend the alleged flow of events to his will. What is left unsaid, of course, is that to
conquer time in that fashion is to employ another set of causal principles. That is, in order to *control* the sequence of events, you must be
able to impose your own order on those events. To do that requires
knowing what is involved in doing so—which amounts to knowing the
causal principles. Silverberg gets away with the illusion of eliminating
causation from his universe only by confusing causal phenomena with
temporal. "In Entropy's Jaws" manages to work, but it does so only at
the expense of trading on this confusion. Thus, Silverberg leaves us
with the illusion of having excised causality, when in fact he has at best
only succeeded in challenging our acceptance of the sequential interpretation of temporal order.

Delaney has no such gambit to rely on in *The Einstein Intersection* and
so is forced to the expedient of allegory to accomplish the same end.
On the surface this is a modern tale of Orpheus. But the story also toys
with the idea of two intersecting universes, each of which operates ac-

cording to different causal principles. While it is an intriguing idea in its inception, Delaney can do nothing with it. The result is a situation in which all apparent regularities concerning human genetics and even death are challenged.

Merely stating that the breakdown in the natural order is brought about by this intersecting of incompatible universes is not the same as making the result plausible. Furthermore, Delaney seems to feel the tension in his own presentation for he ends the book in a most inconclusive fashion. After killing his friend Green-eye and allowing Spider to kill Kid Death, Lobey realizes that he can bring himself back to life, but not Friza, his love. So he decides to take off on some new sort of trip for a while.[7] But before Lobey leaves he and Spider have one last exchange. Spider is speaking:

". . . The Dove leads them in the dance, now, and won't be so ready to forgive you for the choice you made."

"What was it?"

"Between the real and – the rest?"

"Which did I choose?"

Spider pushed my shoulder, grinning. "Maybe you'll know when you get back. Where you off to?" He started to turn.

"Spider?"

He looked back.

"In my village there was a man who grew dissatisfied. So he left this world, worked for a while on the moon, on the outer planets, then on worlds that were stars away. I might go there."

Spider nodded. "I did that once. It was waiting for me when I got back."

"What's it going to be like?"

"It's not going to be what you expect." He grinned, then turned away.

"It's going to be . . . different?"

He kept walking down the sand.

As morning branded the sea, darkness fell away at the far side of the beach. I turned to follow it. (Delaney, p.155)

So the story ends on two somewhat incompatible notes. First, there is the strangely upbeat conclusion to the Orpheus myth. Lobey does not have to remain content with death; he or someone else can bring the dead back to life. Second, despite the fact that Lobey doesn't know what is real anymore, the sense in which the traditional laws of causation are now abrogated remains a mystery.

It does so, moreover, in two senses. First, we have no account given in its place. All we are told (and it is not clear that we are even told this much) is that things will be different. Second, even though Lobey knows he can bring Green-eye back to life, he delays doing so – a point which also signals the end of the familiar Orphean world of traditional causal relations. He delays for a most significant reason – he needs to learn more first. Now this is not only incomprehensible from the point of story development, but is also an admission by Delaney that without a firm grasp on the kinds of laws that are needed to replace our causal orientation, nothing further can be said.[8] As successful storytelling this is a failure. Lack of resolution is not in itself blameworthy, but it is if such a lack follows from a conceptual deadend.

To put it bluntly, *The Einstein Intersection* is a bad book. Its major fault lies in the inability of the author to develop a good idea. Paradoxically, in the very heart of the idea, that which at first blush makes it a good premise, lies the basis of its own inadequacy. The overt theme of the book concerns the state of affairs that results from the imbalance created by the interaction of two incompatible causal contexts. This in itself is not a problem, but the fact that such incompatibility must remain unresolved is.

Let me put this in a slightly different way. To survive, we are required to exert some degree of control over our environment. This is our way of making up for biological inadequacies in size, keenness of sight, speed, strength, etcetera. We have traditionally controlled our environment by mastering what we perceive to be the principles which govern its order and interrelationships. Whether we learn how to first bend the environment to our will and then figure out the principles or vice versa is not important. What is important is that we manage to pass on the information as knowledge. And this particular type of knowledge is a product of the category of causation. It is that feature of our conceptual scheme which makes the very idea of such a set of principles possible.

Our ability to think of the physical world in terms of cause-and-effect relationships between objects is a fact that is constitutive of our understanding of what reality is. To posit another reality lacking the familiar causal behaviors is to ask for one of two things: either we are to suspend any critical judgments concerning the new world or we are to attempt to assimilate that world to our own. In either case we don't have a new *world*. For in those cases where we are asked to suspend critical judgment, there is no way we can continue with any semblance of the cognitive enterprise.

It is one thing to attempt to create the experience of such a novel environment in a film. There we can allow ourselves to sit back and wait for the visual and audio sensations to wash over us. But the very act of reading a book does not permit such passivity. A reader is an active participant in the process of creating a believable situation. If you ask the reader to stop trying to think about the world in familiar terms, you have asked him to stop reading.

If we turn to the other horn of the dilemma and ask the reader to think of the alien world in familiar terms, then we have defeated our purpose. If it is to be an alien world in familiar dress, then we have a story of aliens, not alternative realities.

If, however, we are saying something like, "the laws working in this situation have not yet been discovered, but they will be, so just imagine that something like our causal laws will be the end product," that fails too. And it fails for a reason mentioned earlier—namely, that this could only work by assuming that the same processes operant according to current scientific belief will produce similar results when applied to this problem.

If science is to do the job, then it must be *our* science—that organized activity created by men which examines the limits and depths of our understanding of causal relations between objects. So to imagine another science just won't do.

This is not just an argument for privileged status for some special words like "causation" and "science." It is rather an issue that arises from the way in which we think, must think if you will, about reality. That being the case, it might be argued that there is no necessity for us to think this way—we obviously aren't born thinking this way. So, why can't we change and why can't alternative realities still be possible?

To say that it isn't necessary for us to think this way is to make a strange statement. For on the surface it seems obvious in one sense that we could have been different from the way we are. But that is not really what we are arguing about here. It is not that we could have been different—it is rather that given what we are, can we think about the world in different ways than we now do? Here again it is obvious that indeed people do think differently about the world. (This can be as dramatic a split as the one which is supposed to exist traditionally between East and West, or as mild as the faintly chauvinistic bit of folklore that says women think differently than men.) Furthermore, we see our world today differently than the ancient Greeks conceived of their world. There is no denying that the Greek universe, with its earth standing still in the center, differs from ours. And in terms of cultural activities and human relations, it does not seem inappropriate to refer to it as alien. And yet we can still see the similarity between that world and ours. More than history is involved here. That is, it is not merely the fact that we can trace our development from that world with a sequence of events that makes such understanding possible. For the crux of the matter lies in our ability to understand the Greek reality and this requires more than a sense of historical progression.

The clue lies in the fact that we share a set of fundamental concepts with the Greeks. Let us distinguish with Whewell between a set of general ideas and the manner in which we provide specificity to those ideas.[9] Indeed, how we put the meat on the bones of broad notions is a problem we live with constantly. (An example would be our ongoing efforts to explicate the basic idea inherent in the claim that all men are created equal.)

Now, while we may not view the world and express ourselves in the same specific terms that those of other cultures do, the fact that translations are possible indicates that there is some common framework available. (To wit, to add fractions you need a common base.) I suggest that some of the basic concepts common to the Greeks and ourselves are space, time, causation, appearance, and reality. Furthermore, while a variety of ways exist to work out the specific logics of that set of concepts taken as a unit, it nevertheless follows that that particular set stands together. If you eliminate one of these crucial concepts, you must eliminate at least three others. (The proof of this would make an interesting exercise at this point.)

Assuming that I am right about the necessity of conceptual unity, it seems that our ability to understand the Greeks, or the Japanese, is a matter of our sharing the same conceptual framework. Whether or not this is a genetic result is a question I leave to anyone who can devise a way to test it! But more can be derived from this philosophical perspective. My point is that if a science fiction writer tries to create an alternative universe by tampering with our idea of causation, then he effectively tampers with a number of other fundamental concepts at the same time. If he tries to eliminate one of these concepts without relating it to suitable analogs, then he is simply asking us to chuck out the window our conceptual equipment, our very basis for thought.

Finally, it seems reasonable to ask that if it is impossible to create alternative realities, then what is really being done by all those writers who think they are doing just that? They are confusing true alternative realities with worlds based on new but logically valid relationships between the same fundamental concepts which already make up our conception of this world. In other words, they are making a category mistake. A logical extension and refinement of a conceptual given is not the same as its rejection. Thus, it would be wise for a science fiction writer to do just that—extend the conceptual limits. Furthermore, this should not be confused with another more ambitious but unattainable end, such as developing the basis for a "new consciousness" or other sophomoric misconceptions.

Since this mistake stems from a general confusion as to the requirements of a genuine alternative universe, it is legitimate but no longer excusable. For now that the restraints are clear, I think we can see that in a full-blown alternative, not only will rubber balls not bounce, but if we are really going to tamper with these limits, then most probably they wouldn't exist at all.

5.

Alternative Linguistic Frameworks: Communications with Extraterrestrial Beings

GEORGE F. SEFLER

George Sefler has a broad range of interests in philosophy, having received his training at DePaul University in Chicago, where he graduated Summa Cum Laude (first in a class of over seven hundred degree recipients), and at Georgetown University in Washington, D.C., where he received his doctorate. He has also received a number of postdoctoral fellowships.

Sefler has published an impressive number of articles in a wide variety of journals and has been invited to give presentations to professional organizations all over the country, including the Popular Culture Association Convention in Pittsburgh in 1979, where I invited him to read an earlier draft of the following essay. He argues that any alien language can be translated into an Earth language, at least in principle, though not as Carl Sagan and other scientists have conceived it. Unlike Sagan, Sefler believes that logic, not science, is the universal language. Let us hope that someone at NASA is listening.

Sefler is a professor of philosophy and Dean of the Faculty of Arts and Sciences at Mansfield State College in Pennsylvania, where he has been awarded the Distinguished Teaching Chair, the highest teaching honor bestowed by the Commonwealth of Pennsylvania.

A theme popular in science fiction is man's attempt to communicate with alien civilizations. Like other science fiction plots, this one serves as a device for us to understand the options of our future; it supplies an imaginative exploration into the possible patterns of human communication.

The philosophy of language explores similar areas of concern. And the problem of communication with alien civilizations provides that conceptual point upon which both areas of inquiry converge and at times intersect.

Attempts by astronomers, Carl Sagan, for instance, to send messages into outer space in hopes of communicating with intelligent life forms from other planets provide an immediate practicality and a heightened significance to philosophers' logical explorations into the philosophy of language and science fiction writers' imaginative presentations of alternate alien linguistic frameworks. What are the presuppositional concepts of intelligence necessary for other beings to recognize our signals as such? How would we recognize communication from an alien life form if we received it? Is it possible that communicative signals from other planets have been "received" on earth, yet we have failed to comprehend them because they are linguistic frameworks which are logically untranslatable into human speech?

It may be consoling to note that more often than not science fiction authors portray occasions wherein problems of extraterrestrial communications are overcome. Still, some are pessimistic about contacts with alien civilizations and present the event from the ludicrous (as in Katherine MacLean's "Pictures Don't Lie," in which our visitors from outer space turn out to be so small that they drown in a puddle) to the philosophically intriguing (as in Stanislaw Lem's novel *Solaris*, in which alien civilizations are so different that no commonality for genuine communication with humans seems to exist). It is this latter problem which I wish to discuss. Is it really possible that an alien language is so utterly different that communication is impossible? On what basis could communication be achieved with an alien civilization?

One possible answer is given in the attempt to send a message into outer space on a gold-galvanized aluminum plate attached to Pioneer 10. On it were etched human figures, the locale, epoch, and character of the human builders of Pioneer 10. The presupposition of this etched plate, according to Professor Carl Sagan, is that "it is written in the only language we share with the recipients: Science. . . . The message will be based upon commonalities between the transmitting and receiving civilizations. Those commonalities are, of course, not any spoken or written language or any common instinctual encoding in our genetic materials, but rather what we truly share in common—the universe around us, science, and mathematics."[1]

Certainly, this position is not without support in science fiction. H. Beam Piper in his work "Omnilingual" portrays Martha Dane, a scientist, in her attempt to translate the written works of an extinct Martian civilization. Some of her colleagues question the feasibility of the task, calling the written works of these aliens meaningless. Yet, she is able to make inroads into the lost language through its version of a periodic table of elements. When asked whether the Martian table of elements is anything like the human periodic table, Martha Dane responds, "That isn't just the Martian table of elements; that's *the* table of elements. It's the only one there is. . . ."[2] From this she concluded that "physical science expresses universal facts; necessarily it is a universal language."[3]

The philosophical presupposition here is that scientific or empirical language about the world must always be the same. This means that the world, the cosmos, is intelligible in itself, independent of any language. Consequently, empirical language is purely passive; it is a mirroring of the articulated character inherent in things. Empirical language reflects the structures already present in things. Facts of the world constitute the ultimate independent foundation of empirical language and of truth itself. Thus, the philosopher W. V. Quine summarizes Piper's and Sagan's views by stating that "empirical meaning is what remains when . . . we peel away the verbiage. It is what the sentences of one language and their firm translations in a completely alien language have in common."[4]

I maintain that this view is suspect. There is no absolute gulf between the empirical and the conceptual. The issue is not whether there exists some external physical world, but whether this world comes linguistically prearticulated as we know it, or whether empirical language is in some way a construction of, a shaping of, the stuff of experience according to certain human structures.

This doesn't mean that the world of nature is a conglomerate of mental images; there is more to the world than one's own conscious perceptions. Yet, perceptions are more than passive observations, and empirical language is more than mirroring and reporting statements. The world does not provide an independent foundation to either language or experience; it is not independently intelligible. The famous philosopher of language Ludwig Wittgenstein states:

> It might be imagined that some propositions, of the form of empirical propositions, were hardened and functioned as channels for such empirical propositions as were not hardened but fluid; and that this relation altered with time, in that fluid propositions hardened and hard ones became fluid.[5]

Certain linguistic forms are so rock-bottom fundamental to language activities that they have become the rules for those activities. "Isn't what I am saying: any empirical proposition can be transformed into a postulate," states Wittgenstein, "and then becomes a norm of description."[6]

Empirical descriptions, factual utterances, are nothing more than generally accepted interpretations. Descriptive propositions are not absolutely distinct from nondescriptive ones. And actual statements do not directly reveal something about the world; directly, they reveal something about the structures through which these propositions organize the world and then they describe it through such structures.

Thus Quine, comparing physical objects to the gods of Homer, concludes that "in point of epistemological footing, the physical objects and the gods differ only in degree and not in kind. Both sorts of entities enter our conception only as cultural posits."[7]

In the antiquated view that the universe came prepackaged in thing-like categories, the prime concern of language was to record such demarcations; a globally alternate language system was an impossibility. Yet if we accept the above notions, this view becomes questionable; following from the Sapir-Whorf hypothesis, indications are that languages carve up the world in different ways. Theoretically, then, the possibility exists that one communications system can segment reality in a way so totally different from another system that together they defy intertranslation. Respectively, these would be *alternate linguistic frameworks,* which hereafter will be called ALFs. Alien languages would seem to be prime sources for such alternate frameworks, and as such the possibility of extraterrestrial communication would be called into question.

I agree with the philosophical analysis that empirical propositions are basically interpretational and thus alien civilizations and human civilization might not share a common factual world. But I do not think this means that there can exist an alternate linguistic framework. As a philosopher, I maintain that an ALF is not a real option. I argue that an ALF is a logical impossibility; it is a misconception of language to speak of a totally untranslatable language from a logical, or *a priori*, viewpoint.

Professor Richard Rorty suggests that an alternate conceptual framework can be understood as a system in which all our true beliefs are false.[8] Such a system would indeed be different from ours, yet to speak of false beliefs (and likewise, by implication, false propositions) as the basis of an ALF is to cloud the issue. Utterances in a language system untranslatable into human speech are not false, but meaningless.

Hypothetically speaking, in response to someone or something speaking to us in an untranslatable language (or one which we do not know how to translate), we can at best shrug our shoulders and admit noncomprehension. Whereas, a language system which is globally false in human speech is obviously translatable into the latter so that its falsity can be determined. And in response to a statement made in this globally distinct framework, one can say, "I understand what you are saying but I disagree with it." That is, I know what would be the case if what you said is true, but I do not find it to be the case.

Moreover, it is conceivable that a person systematically uses language such that all his statements are false, and yet his speech could be intelligible. One can understand someone perfectly well without knowing the truth of his statements; propositions make sense independently of our knowing their truth or falsity. The latter is an empirical issue; the former, logical. An ALF is radically distinct from our own linguistic framework; it cannot be understood therein. Whereas, a person can certainly make himself understood by false propositions. In fact, this is precisely what occurs in the language of lying.

Logically, then, linguistic frameworks cannot be distinguished on the grounds of the truth or falsity of propositions in their respective alternates. The real question is whether a language is necessarily meaningless from the perspective of another language. ALFs are not determined by their content, that is, how things are, but by the forms of the language, namely, that things can be said in one language which are *a priori* not sayable in another. The ultimate test is the form of the propositions—is a language structure *a priori* meaningless at a global level from the perspective of another framework?

To answer this question in the affirmative is to misconceive language. However, one can say that in a limited area the situation holds. For example, the wave theory of light cannot describe light as a corpuscle, and vice versa. But, globally, this doesn't make them ALFs since both the wave and the corpuscle characters of light are explainable in the language of physics. An ALF would be more akin to a physical phenomenon that can never be explained in the language of physics. This would imply some necessary restrictions within man's language which would make it unreceptive to a certain state of affairs. But our language doesn't have such *a priori* restrictions.

Borrowing an image from Wittgenstein, let us think of language as a toolbox. The kinds of language uses are as diverse as tools. More important, there is no set limit as to the kinds of tools that can exist, apart from any logical restrictions. So also with language, because of its open-ended character, no *a priori* limits are built into the system, at least globally speaking. Logically, the possibility of an untranslatable language or an alternate conceptual framework simply cannot exist, since it would view a language as a closed system, a complete system wherein one has reached the absolute limits of usage. My conclusion, then, is that ALFs cannot exist; I say this apart from any direct empirical considerations.

Of course, it could be argued that aliens are not present here and now to challenge this claim. But this is logically irrelevant since to speak of alternate linguistic frameworks is really to talk about our own language and not the aliens'. To be possible means to be somehow incorporatable into our language system. To speak of the possibility of an ALF is really to ask: does it make sense in our language to speak of an ALF? Obviously, the answer is no. The alternate framework cannot be totally incommensurable, otherwise it would not be recognizable as a linguistic framework.[9]

Often on the "Star Trek" television series Dr. Spock encounters some alien form. Checking out his sensor device, Spock informs Captain Kirk that these readings indicate a life form *totally* alien to life as we know it. This is a misuse of language; if it is totally alien to life forms as we know them, why call it a life form? In such language, the term "life form" is not given any meaning.

A similar situation occurs with the term "alternate linguistic framework." If it is a totally alien framework, it is arbitrary to call it a linguistic framework; the term is not given any intelligible meaning. Differences make sense only within a framework, but totally alternate frameworks deny such a common base. Thus, on a logical basis, failure of total intertranslatability is the key to alternate linguistic frameworks. Yet such a total intertranslatability as a necessary requisite presupposes recognition of something as a linguistic framework. This entails some overlapping character to designate it intelligibly as a linguistic framework; but it is such a character which *a priori* is denied in an ALF.

There is still another problem, an empirical one: even though an ALF is a logical impossibility, there can exist very real problems in translating an alien language. Although, as I have argued, such a translation would not be a logical impossibility, it could prove an empirical "impossibility." An alien language might be untranslatable because we simply have not found the translation key, but this does not constitute a proof that such a translation cannot be found. Unsuccessful attempts at translating an alien language would not prove it to be an ALF; there always exists the possibility that one did not go far enough in searching out the translation.

In conclusion, communication with alien civilizations, unlike Stanislaw Lem's *Solaris* would indicate, is an ongoing possibility. Both we earthlings and the aliens do have a point of reference, a common foundation for communication. But this base would not necessarily be science or any other empirical base. Even though this communication might be sense observable or empirical to the one communicant, there is no assurance that the other shares this basis; the communication can be a deductive construct for the aliens or vice versa.

Yet the communication is in common as a communication, and this is discerned in terms of its structured or logical character. Even for empirical knowledge to be possible, there must be presupposed a logical framework. A description of the world is not given as *a priori* true; rather, logically speaking there are needed principles in terms of which statements assume meaning. It is in the possibility of sharing these principles that the common base for extraterrestrial communication is founded.

6.

Omnilinguals

PETER BARKER

Peter Barker received his bachelor's degree with honors in physics and philosophy at Oxford and then came to the United States to complete his doctorate in philosophy at the State University of New York at Buffalo, with a dissertation on Albert Einstein's philosophy of science. His areas of professional specialization include philosophy of science, philosophy of language, British empiricism, and the philosophy of Wittgenstein. His interests in Einstein continue, as exemplified in his collaboration on a distinguished collection of essays (After Einstein: Proceedings of the Einstein Centennial Celebration), *one of which will be his own, "Einstein's Later Philosophy of Science." Barker is also the assistant editor of the* Southern Journal of Philosophy.

The following essay concerns the possibility of translating alien languages into those of terrestrial origin. Unlike Sefler, Barker believes that it is quite conceivable that an alien language would be incapable of translation, for there may exist no shared conceptual framework between the users of the alien language and those of terrestrial languages. Interesting parallels are

drawn between encountering an alien language and
judging the revolutions in the history of science.
Barker is now an associate professor of philosophy
at Memphis State University, where he has taught since
1975.

Science fiction is so prolific in its philosophical interests that it sometimes anticipates new philosophical ideas. In the special area of philosophy called "philosophy of science," the most important new ideas of the last twenty years can be traced to a book by Thomas Kuhn called *The Structure of Scientific Revolutions*.[1]

The theme of the book is that science is not a cumulative enterprise which progresses by piling new successes on old ones, but that occasionally scientific revolutions occur, when all the old successes are thrown out and a completely new pile is started. When Kuhn's book was published in 1962, this idea startled the people who call themselves philosophers of science. But both the old cumulative view of science and the new noncumulative view were already part of science fiction literature.

I will illustrate some of the important features of the new noncumulative view of science with quotations from science fiction, so that I may use this idea to address a major philosophical problem: the first contact problem. Although philosophers have long discussed the nature of science, the serious discussion of the first contact problem has taken place almost exclusively in science fiction literature.

The first contact problem is the problem of setting up communication on first contact with extraterrestrial life. This problem may be subdivided into two separate problems, corresponding to the questions: "How do I know that he, she, or it is *worth* talking to?" and "How do I talk to it?"

I call the corresponding problems the *identification problem* and the *communication problem*. Both problems clearly have philosophical aspects.

The identification problem can be read as a request for an analysis of the concept of intelligence which will apply to both humans and nonhumans. The communication problem raises issues about translation and the limits of the concept of language, which have recently occupied the attention of many analytic philosophers.

To be philosophically scrupulous for a moment, I will only be examining one aspect of the first contact problem. I will be concerned only with the communication problem, although the solutions to both aspects of the first contact problem are obviously connected. Everything I have to say assumes that the identification problem has already been settled and that we are in the position of attempting to set up communication with a group of aliens already identified as intelligent.[2] My main purpose will be to argue that establishing communication may be very much harder than is frequently assumed. I will consider three possible ways of establishing communication: by shared cultural patterns, by science, and by mathematics.

By shared cultural patterns, the first possibility, I mean simply that the aliens do the work for us. Around the world, normal radio and television broadcasts are interrupted by a message from space: "People of Earth! We are the Timekeepers from the Planet Remulak. Your weapons are useless against us. . . ." Examples of this scenario range from the Koneheads of NBC's "Saturday Night Live" to Arthur Clarke's first great novel, *Childhood's End*. The aliens generally are depicted as older and wiser than humans. From their announcement it is clear that they have already translated our languages, so we can communicate with them in plain English or Russian or whatever.

I want to dismiss this possibility quickly for two reasons. First, even if the aliens have translated our languages, we still need to translate theirs, so in an important sense the communication problem remains.[3] Second, if human difficulties in translating alien languages arise from cultural dissimilarities, these difficulties will work in both directions; the aliens will probably be unable to translate our languages without our help.

The major obstacle to approaching the translation of an alien language in the way we might approach an unknown human language is the possible absence of common cultural patterns. When a human explorer approaches a newly discovered human culture, the members of that culture have a certain minimum of things in common with the explorer. At the purely physiological level members of the culture will require food, drink, sleep, and sex. These requirements will be embodied in cultural patterns or institutions: finding or preparing food, finding or preparing shelter, and so on. If members of the culture bake bread and build houses, an explorer who is familiar with these activities from his own society can participate in the corresponding native activities and begin to learn their language.

When the nonverbal aspects of the communication problem are settled, all that is required to establish verbal communication is a little patience and ingenuity. I can help you build a house even if I cannot talk to you about it, provided we generally agree on the process involved. Having reached the point where we can cooperate in housebuilding, it should be a simple matter for me to learn the vocabulary you associate with it and vice versa.

So the problem that arises in translating a nonhuman language is that there may simply be no shared cultural patterns – the aliens may require neither food nor shelter. There may indeed be no common elements in the everyday behavior of members of the two races. In such a situation the usual pattern of translation breaks down.[4]

I am going to lump together all the techniques that have been used in the past to translate unknown human languages and assume that they will fail us. I want to examine two more alternatives which have never, as far as I know, been used as the key to human languages, but which have been proposed in science fiction as possible techniques for translating alien languages.

However different we are physically and culturally, we must have at least one "cultural pattern" in common with any alien race capable of interstellar travel, and that is science.

As a second possibility, then, consider using science itself as the basis for translating an alien language. H. Beam Piper constructed a story around this single idea.[5] Arriving on Mars, a group of explorers discover that the natives died out a few thousand years in the past, leaving behind a mass of well-preserved artifacts and buildings, complete with inscriptions and pictures. The language of the dead Martians defies all attempts to translate it until one of the explorers discovers a wall chart which can only be the periodic table of the elements. The periodic table then becomes the "Rosetta Stone" which keys Martian to English.

Given a working vocabulary of more than one hundred words, the expedition proceeds to translate the language, starting with the books on physics and chemistry.

The idea that science is an "omnilingual" or a universal language (or at least a universal key to translation) is an attractive one. It is implicit in almost all science fiction treatments of the first contact problem. However bizarre or incomprehensible human explorers find alien cultures and customs, they are generally depicted as understanding the alien's science. In nonfiction terms the same idea motivated the design of the plaque aboard Pioneer 10, to be deciphered by future interceptors of the spacecraft, as well as the messages which have been prepared for radio transmission to distant civilizations.

There is one fundamental difficulty with this idea – the phenomenon of the scientific revolution, which has recently become one of the centers of interest in philosophy of science and has led to a major revision in how philosophers describe science. As I suggested earlier, both the old view of science (which these new developments replaced) and the new view can be found in science fiction. According to the old view, science is a cumulative phenomenon which grows by adding new knowledge to old and established knowledge. According to the new view, science periodically undergoes noncumulative changes – scientific revolutions – during which old, established knowledge is eliminated and new and incompatible knowledge replaces it.

The treatment of interstellar travel in science fiction illustrates these two views of science. If Einstein is right and the speed of light cannot be exceeded, interstellar travel becomes a very time-consuming business for humans. Ursula Le Guin has constructed a future history which accepts this limitation. Most authors, however, find a way around Einstein, either by wrapping their starships in a space-warp in which Einstein's principles do not apply, or by removing the ship completely from ordinary ("Einsteinian") space into "sub-space" or "hyperspace."

From a philosophical viewpoint all these suggestions share a common feature – they assume that Einstein must be right in the areas of knowledge claimed by his theories ("normal space") and that to circumvent the speed of light limitation we must discover a new area of knowledge (warp- , sub- , or hyper-space) where the rules we have already discovered do not apply.

A refined version of this view is presented by Larry Niven and Jerry Pournelle in *The Mote in God's Eye*.[6] They assume that the scientific laws we have already discovered are correct, but only in the region where the discoveries were made. Close to stars the laws of science are as we know them, but in interstellar space they are completely different. Adding these new laws allows faster-than-light travel using the Addison drive, but only in the regions where the new laws apply.

The view of science which underlies these stories is conservative — once a theory has become well-established it will never be eliminated, although it may need to be qualified. Science is the accumulation of such theories and qualifications.

But there is a much more dramatic way to make room for faster-than-light travel. When James Blish sets up his future history in *A Case of Conscience*, he introduces a physicist called Haertel who provided

> . . . that description of the space-time continuum which, by swallowing up the Lorentz-Fitzgerald contraction exactly as Einstein had Swallowed Newton (that is alive) had made interstellar flight possible.[7]

Blish's central character looks at science as "an endless series of theoretical catastrophes." One of these catastrophes has provided him with faster-than-light travel. The catastrophe was a scientific revolution which swept away the theories that forbade exceeding the speed of light.

During revolutions science grows noncumulatively. Old established theories are discarded in favor of new and incompatible ones. Although, as Blish says, we have the impression that Einstein swallowed Newton alive, from an ontological viewpoint the prospects of this sort of afterlife are not attractive. If the universe is constructed out of the entities required by Einstein's theories — continuous fields — there is no room for Newton's fundamental entities, which are point particles. From a logical viewpoint if we accept Einstein's laws as true, we must admit that Newton's laws are false. The limiting case relationship which permits the recovery of Newton's laws from Einstein's (which shows, if you like, how he was "swallowed alive") requires that the Einsteinian prediction of any physical effect always differs from the Newtonian one.

The replacement of an established theory by a new and incompatible one leads to great difficulties in understanding and accepting the new theory from the old viewpoint. Blish's character quoted above goes on to reflect that he does not understand a word of Haertel's new theory, although, "it was doubtless perfectly simple. . . ." Many distinguished physicists who were trained during the period when Newton's theories were held without question simply never accepted Einstein's work. A notorious example is Ernst Mach, who never accepted Einstein, though Einstein regarded him as a source of inspiration.

My favorite description of the failure of communication brought on by scientific revolution comes from A. E. Van Vogt's "Far Centaurus."[8] In this story four astronauts set out for Centaurus at sublight speed in suspended animation. During the four hundred years they are in transit, a scientific revolution occurs, faster-than-light travel becomes common, and they arrive to discover that the Centaurus system has already been colonized for several centuries. One of the locals tries to explain the force which propels his starships:

> "The adeledicnander force," said Cassellahat. "I've been trying to explain it to Mr. Renfrew, but his mind seems to balk at some of the most simple aspects."
> Renfrew roused himself, grimaced. "He's been trying to tell me that electrons think; and I won't swallow it."
> Cassellahat shook his head. "Not think; they don't think. But they have a psychology."
> "Electronic psychology!" I said.
> "Simple adeledicnander," Cassellahat replied. "Any child —"
> Renfrew groaned: "I know. Any child of six could tell me."

This illustrates a characteristic problem associated with scientific revolutions. People on one side of a revolution may be quite incapable of understanding people on the other side — they may even fail to recognize that what goes on after the revolution is still science.

Let me underline this point by discussing something that any child of six could tell you today, from the viewpoint of someone trained in another scientific era. Consider the claim that the Earth is a planet. When Copernicus made this suggestion, the accepted cosmological theory was that of Aristotle. Aristotle's universe is divided into two concentric parts: the heavens or celestial realm and the earth or terrestrial realm. The sum of these parts constitutes all that exists and the parts are mutually exclusive. To say that something is part of the celestial realm excludes the possibility that it can be part of the terrestrial realm and vice versa.

Consider, then, an Aristotelian analysis of Copernicus' basic idea "The Earth is a planet."

1. Planets are part of the heavens, or that which is celestial.
2. That which is celestial is that which is not terrestrial.

By definition, not to mention common sense:

3. The Earth is that which is terrestrial.

So the claim "The Earth is a planet" can be analyzed as "That which is terrestrial (the Earth) is that which is not terrestrial (a planet)," which is a clear contradiction. Without even considering observational evidence, we can reject Copernicus' theory on the grounds that his idea is false on logical grounds alone. It is not surprising if some of Copernicus' Aristotelian contemporaries thought he had not advanced science but abandoned it.

The difficulties in using science as a universal language should be clear. Science undergoes large-scale noncumulative changes. Examples are the transition from Aristotle to Newton, from Newton to Einstein and, in Blish's story, from Einstein to Haertel. Science can only form a basis for translation if we happen to encounter the aliens at a point in their scientific history parallel to our own. If they are going through an Einsteinian period while we are accepting some successor (like Haertel), the difficulties in establishing communication on the basis of science will be just as great as those associated with ordinary translation techniques.

Even this is a simplification. There is no reason to think that the alien's science must progress through just the same sequence of revolutions as our own. At least some of the causes of scientific development, and hence scientific revolutions, are extrascientific (think of the influence of Pearl Harbor on our understanding of atomic energy). Different cultures will exert different influences producing different sequences of revolutions. Imagine that the alien's equivalent of the ancient Greeks developed an exact science of psychology rather than an exact science of astronomy, as in our case.

It seems perfectly possible to imagine an alien culture proceeding from a different starting point through different scientific revolutions to a set of theories which we have never come across. To the extent that our science reflects our culture and history it is no more useful as a starting point for communication than any other aspect of our culture and history.[9]

Perhaps the solution to the communication problem is to be found by looking for a part of language which is completely free of cultural or historical influences. Mathematics and logic are obvious candidates. Mathematics has been suggested as a possible basis for communication with aliens in many science fiction stories. This represents the third possibility which I will deal with only briefly.[10]

Almost the same argument I have made against the possibility of using science as a basis for translation can be made in the case of mathematics. Mathematics, too, is a product of individual cultures. Mathematics goes through stages of noncumulative growth which may hinder communication between people with different views.

For example, geometry was discovered by the ancient Greeks, algebra and the concept of zero were invented by the Arabs, and calculus was invented in Europe in the seventeenth century. The Greeks would probably have refused to recognize calculus as a branch of mathematics. They possessed clearly articulated and strongly held prejudices against the concept of infinity, which enters essentially into the use of calculus. Similarly, they would probably have refused to recognize algebra as mathematics on the grounds that zero was not a number (any more than the Earth was a planet).

Alien mathematics may be as different from our own as our mathematics is from the Greeks'. This idea is suggested in the closing pages of Ursula Le Guin's *City of Illusions*. One of the central questions in the plot is whether the Earth has been successfully invaded by an alien race, the Shing. The central character unmasks the aliens and is provided with his final piece of evidence as he prepares a starship for his escape:

> Remarren . . . went straight to the computers and set to work. He already knew from his examination of the onboard controls that the mathematics involved in some of the ship's operations was not the familiar . . . mathematics which Terrans still used and from which [his own] mathematics, via the Colony, also derived. Some of the processes the Shing used and built into their computers were entirely alien to [human] mathematical process and logic; and nothing else could have so firmly persuaded Remarren that the Shing were, indeed, alien to Earth, alien to all the [human] worlds, conquerors from some very distant world. He had never been quite sure that Earth's old histories and tales were correct on that point, but now he was convinced. He was, after all, essentially a mathematician.[11]

So perhaps even the mathematician cannot help us. I have now eliminated three possibilities for translating an alien language: the standard translation technique which rests on identification of shared cultural patterns, and two nonstandard techniques taking either science or mathematics as a translation key. If all these fail, is anything left?

All three techniques share the assumption that an alien language must be understood by translating it into a language we already understand. Not all languages are understood in this way, however. The first language we learned, our native language, obviously was not acquired by translating it into a language we already knew. At the risk of tautology: before we learned our first language we did not know any! The processes of first and second language acquisition are quite separate and distinct. Only after we have acquired our first language is it possible for us to acquire second and subsequent languages by translation.

Perhaps the right way to approach an alien language is as a first language acquisition problem. This raises difficulties for an adult. It is not clear that an adult could ever successfully set aside a language already acquired and learn an alien language as the aliens themselves learn it. A further difficulty is that it seems the acquisition of our first language involves unrepeatable physical processes which take place before the age of six or not at all.[12] Fortunately these processes are not limited to one language. Many children of western missionaries to China mastered both English and Chinese before the age of six.

So perhaps the solution to communicating with aliens is to provide them with a child to be brought up in contact with both linguistic communities and to serve as a translator. The central character of Robert Heinlein's *Stranger in a Strange Land* had just such an experience and came away much the better for it.[13]

In case you think this solves the problem, in closing I would remind you that at least one nonhuman species on Earth seems to be intelligent and may even possess a language—the dolphins. Clearly we cannot establish communication with the dolphins by giving them a baby to bring up. However, this suggestion indicates the limitations of first language acquisition as a communication technique.[14]

7.

Could Anyone Here Speak Babel-17?

WILLIAM M. SCHUYLER, JR.

William Schuyler, Jr. received his bachelors degree from the University of Illinois with honors in mathematics and distinction in philosophy, earning memberships in three national honoraries: Phi Beta Kappa, Phi Kappa Phi, and Phi Mu Epsilon (in mathematics). He did his graduate study at Princeton in the history and philosophy of science, earning his masters degree in 1962, after receiving fellowships from Phi Kappa Phi, the Woodrow Wilson Foundation, and the National Science Foundation. The next year, he accepted a position in the philosophy department at the University of Louisville, where he is now an associate professor.

The following essay, a draft of which he presented to the Popular Culture Association Convention in Pittsburgh in 1979, argues that Samuel Delany's imagined language, Babel-17, is not a possible one. Schuyler's criticism tells us much about the prerequisites of natural languages.

Samuel R. Delany's *Babel-17* has been a favorite of mine ever since the first time I read it. My admiration for the book's style and its content have not ceased to grow. However, it is not my purpose here to discuss eternal literary values or my impeccable taste; nor shall I be concerned with literary or philosophical influences, or the place of this book in the author's life or literary development.

Embedded in the book is a philosophical position I want to examine. The position is complex, its implications wide-ranging, its details ingenious and elegant. My question is, is it tenable?

The possibility of a language with the characteristics of Babel-17 rests on certain assumptions about the human mind, the nature of knowledge, and the ways in which we can know. By examining some characteristics attributed to the language, we bring these assumptions to light. That will be my first task, for they are the heart of the philosophical position. My second will be to determine whether the position is sound and the language possible.

Since Delany is a good writer, he doesn't usually harangue us or allow his characters to do so. Hence much of the position must be inferred from what happens. It's easy to go wrong at this kind of inference, but I think I can provide adequate justification for attributing to Delany the position I am going to describe.

Philosophers of language have in recent years been concerned with problems about reference: how do the words I use enable you to identify what I'm talking about? In particular, referring to oneself is of interest because of its relation to the problem of specifying the conditions under which awareness of oneself is possible.

When we first encounter the Butcher, he speaks English,[1] but his style is odd. He does not understand the word *I*. He cannot even refer to himself indirectly, although he can refer to others and knows when he is addressed by name. He also does not recognize other people as persons; he lacks that concept altogether.[2]

Is this possible? Self-reference by circumlocution is easy enough to manage in English. Why must the Butcher bang on his chest with his fist?[3] Because it does not occur to him to refer to himself.

The Butcher is in effect a native speaker of Babel-17. That is, he had his memory wiped and was then taught Babel-17 as his "first" language. It does not occur to him to refer to himself because Babel-17 lacks the concepts of self and other, as well as that of person.[4] If it's not in the language, you can't think it (unless you expand the language).[5]

Rydra Wong eventually does expand the language.[6] It would seem that self-reference was not logically impossible in Babel-17; it was just that the possibility was not made actual.

But surely that's too simple. Babel-17 is subtle, flexible, and very complex. How could it lack something as basic as the distinction between self and other? I think the answer is that it is based on a mode of cognition, a way or style of knowing, which is radically different from those presupposed by the natural languages with which we are familiar.

In fact, Babel-17 forces a mode of cognition on its speakers.[7] Not only that, " 'but language is thought. Thought is information given form. The form is language.' "[8] So the language and the mode of cognition, if they are not identical (which is an open question), have at the very least the same form. Whatever we can infer about the form of one is true of the other. So it is legitimate here to shift back and forth between language and mode of cognition, because we are exploring Delany's position and he has licensed such transitions. Elsewhere it might be otherwise.

The mode is a form of gestalt perception in which everything in one's experience is integrated into a unitary whole. The linguistic counterpart of this mode of cognition is already familiar to philosophers—it is known as the picture theory of meaning, and its thesis is that a sentence *means* in the same way that a picture *depicts*.

One of the problems with pictures as a means of communication is that they do not have a mechanism for focusing attention. If you show me a picture, how can I tell what it is that you want to point out to me? Is it the colors? The composition? The action going on in the lower left-hand corner? In other words, how can you refer?

In fact, you can't. Now we can see the real reason for the Butcher's problem. His mode of cognition, reflected in his language, has no way to focus on part of a gestalt, hence no way to distinguish between self and other. This appears in his language as an inability to refer to himself. It's not that he just didn't think of it; his way of thinking does not permit it.

But if the Butcher's mode of cognition does not permit a distinction between self and other, how can he function at all? It would seem that he should have no concept of action, as that would require the notion of a self to be the actor. He could react without self-awareness, but surely that isn't enough to account for everything he does.

The answer is simple, but odd. He may not make the distinction between self and other, but he can still have a concept of self. He will not perceive himself as distinct from the rest of the world; he will perceive a gestalt. As far as he is concerned, he *is* this pattern he perceives – all of it. The pattern is the self. Insofar as he can conceive of being an individual, he will think of himself as the whole pattern – his physical self will not be bounded by the surface of his body. Thus he can conceive of action, but only in terms of the pattern acting to alter itself. Of course, he still can't refer, and the ability to focus is still missing. We still need to ask whether he could function in such a state.

Delany's answer is very bold and has far-reaching implications. Focus is necessary only because you might miss something due to inefficient cognitive processing or because you could fail to recognize the relevance or significance of something. If you are using Babel-17, and hence the mode of cognition that goes with it, you get all the information that is available. The very structure of the language forces the mode of cognition on the speaker, and the mode of cognition forces awareness of every detail, which makes it impossible to miss patterns and connections.[9]

These are good grounds for saying that Babel-17 is a picture-language but they should be supplemented by considerations more closely tied to the text. Consider Wong's solution to the problem posed by the first act of sabotage to her ship. In explaining how she reached the solution, she practically tells us that Babel-17 is a picture-language:

> "Great Circle" carries some information with it, but not the right information to get us out of the jam we're in. We have to go to another language in order to think about the problem clearly without going through all sorts of roundabout paths for the proper aspects of what we want to deal with.[10]

Could it be that Babel-17 just happens to carry the right information to deal with this incident?

Apparently not. In every case where she uses Babel-17, exactly the right information is available. I simply do not believe that Delany meant us to understand this as a series of remarkable coincidences. The clear inference is that if you speak the language, all the information you need to solve a problem will be explicitly built into your description of it. Since we cannot anticipate what problems we might encounter, it follows that all the information there is, or at least all that is known, about something is explicitly presented when it is mentioned. This kind of explicit presentation is characteristic of pictures. (Or at any rate, it is characteristic of some of them. For others, we need to know a context. I shall have more to say about contexts hereafter.)

Conversely, English is not adequate to describe some of the things Wong does in Babel-17. In naming the webbing which holds her in her hammock, she learns how to break it; but Delany is unable to describe adequately how she went about naming it. In the commons of Jebel Tarik, she is, as far as I can tell, simultaneously aware of everything; and once again Delany fails—brilliantly—to convey the requisite impression. He fails because language has failed him.[11]

I suggest that this is true for the same reason that natural language is not adequate for the representation of pictures. Pictures show, and so do their proper parts. A proper part here would be, say, a piece of a painting; but not the canvas without the paint, or all and only the red paint. In a painting the proper part is like the whole.

On the other hand, assuming that words are the proper parts of sentences,[12] whatever words do in sentences is not the same as what sentences do. For one thing, there are several kinds of words, where there is only one kind of proper part of a picture. Different kinds of words will have different functions, so whatever the function of a sentence, they cannot *all* have that function, if indeed *any* of them do. In a sentence, the proper parts are not like the whole; hence sentence and picture are incommensurable.

How do the proper parts of Babel-17 act? The first step is to identify them.

She *something* at *something*. The first something was a tiny vocable that implied an immediate, but passive, perception that could be aural or ol-

factory as well as visual. The second something was three equally tiny
phonemes that blended at different musical pitches: one, an indicator
that fixed the size of the chamber at twenty-five feet long and roughly
cubical, the second identifying the color and probable substance of the
walls—some blue metal—while the third was at once a place holder for
particles that should denote the room's functions when she discovered
it, and a sort of grammatical tag by which she could refer to the whole
experience with only the one symbol for as long as she needed.[13]

This is the fullest discussion I can find of the structure of Babel-17.
Though it is brief and incomplete, it does provide enough information
to identify the proper parts of Babel-17.

The things that Delany mentions in his discussion of Babel-17 may
not be proper parts of it, for parts can carry information without being
proper parts. Letters as such, for example, are not words, nor are they
proper parts of English sentences. Nevertheless, an English word is
written as a string of letters, and from that string we can determine
what the word is. Hence the letters must carry information of some
kind.

Similarly, phonemes or vocables cannot be proper parts of Babel-17.
In discussing the "second something," Delany says that its phonemes
are blended. This must be more than an observation about phonetics.
From the context, it means that, like the notation which Wong constructed for the concept of a great circle, only the whole "second something" has meaning, even though the phonemes carry information.
The analogy holds because Wong constructed the great circle notation
under the influence of Babel-17.[14] So, if anything in the discussion of
the language is a proper part of Babel-17, it is the "somethings," not the
phonemes.

Yet the "somethings" cannot be proper parts either, even though we
can describe them in English. Their description shows that they are not
complete in themselves: they must be combined to get a complete utterance. They are different in kind from complete utterances and from
each other. But the Butcher cannot make distinctions of kind. He perceives only gestalts. Gestalts may be larger or smaller in scope, but the
only proper parts of gestalts are themselves gestalts, just as a proper
part of a picture is itself a picture. Since the mode of cognition here reflects, and is reflected in, the language, the Butcher could not grasp the

"somethings," for they are incomplete and therefore cannot represent gestalts or proper parts of gestalts. What the Butcher could understand would be a representation of a gestalt or a proper part of a gestalt. But a proper part of a gestalt is itself a gestalt, so a representation of one would be a representation of a gestalt and thus complete in itself, which the "somethings" are not. In other words, the proper parts of complete utterances in Babel-17 must be things that by themselves could be complete utterances.[15]

Thus, none of the ways which Delany uses to distinguish parts of Babel-17 divides utterances in that language into proper parts. This is because proper parts of utterances in Babel-17 act like parts of pictures rather than parts of sentences in natural language. The conjecture is now proven: Babel-17 must be a picture-language.

A mode of cognition must relate to the world. Are these perceived gestalts images of something in the world or are they something we impose on the world? I think Delany's position is that there are patterns in the world. One reason is that our perception of patterns can be passive, as in the incident where Wong breaks the webbing in the sickbay. What she perceives there is pattern, the stress pattern of the net; and since she perceives it passively, she cannot be imposing it. Another reason is that Babel-17 is a picture-language. Since it can be freed of bias, it becomes a way of knowing the world as it really is. Metaphysics will become an exact science.[16]

There's just one small catch to this. Depiction is a relation between a picture and what is pictured. Specifically, it is the one which holds between utterances in Babel-17 and the states of affairs which those utterances represent. In order for Babel-17 to work as it is supposed to, the depiction relation must not allow addition, change, or deletion of information in the transition from what is pictured to picture, from state of affairs to utterance. So Babel-17 is possible only if we can perceive the world as it really is. But what if the mind has filters built in as original equipment which cannot be removed? We might then be unable to determine not only what has been filtered out, but also the original form of the information that has gotten past the filters. Roughly speaking, that was Kant's position.

Two kinds of evidence suggest that Delany would reject a Kantian position. First, Wong is a telepath who can read the minds of animals as well as humans, which shows that she is capable of perceiving and understanding nonlinguistic mental processes. This should be seen as a kind of direct perception of the world. Second, the discorporates, who have neither sense organs nor brains, are able to perceive. They do put their perceptions in sensory terms to communicate with the living, but no doubt they are speaking metaphorically. This suggests that the discorporates have immediate perceptions of space and matter, even if the living do not.[17]

Now, if there are direct or immediate perceptions, which is the position Delany takes, then by definition they cannot have been made through filters. Indeed, it seems that direct perception is always possible in the context he has constructed. It follows that the kind of depiction relation needed for Babel-17 is possible. The catch has not caught Delany.

So, we have a picture-language and a gestalt mode of cognition which have remarkable properties. Indeed, they are said to be very close to a maximally efficient way of using human mental capacities.[18] But do humans actually have the mental capacities required for Babel-17? I shall argue that they do not.

In language, there is a trade-off: the more explicit information given, the longer the message. The usual strategy for avoiding excessively long messages is to let a great deal remain implicit. But if too much is left unsaid the message will not be understood. So you can trade brevity for clarity and vice versa.

What can be left unsaid depends on the audience. This is true among users of a single language, but there are even more radical differences among speakers of different languages. To learn another language is also to learn other conventions about what may be left implicit and what must be made explicit.[19]

Is anything left implicit in Babel-17? I don't think the text is entirely clear on this point. We have seen mention of tags which can be used to refer to experiences without calling up complete descriptions, and of place holders for missing information. We are not told whether known information can be left out. However if it could, there would be a method of focusing attention, and apparently there isn't. The tags, which seem to function somewhat like names, provide a method of leaving information implicit, but they are no more than a form of abbreviation. The deleted information can be recovered as long as one can recall what was abbreviated.

It is stipulated that Babel-17 is a very compact language. Even so, could we really be conscious of all the information we could get? Let us grant that we need not be aware of all of it at once. Could we leave enough out of an utterance in Babel-17 about, say, elementary number theory so that we can utter it in a finite length of time? Or, to put it another way, would we have to be conscious of an infinite number of numbers and mathematical truths every time we thought about elementary number theory?

Any answer to these last two questions would violate some claim about the necessary properties of Babel-17. If we must be conscious of an infinite number of numbers and theorems when we think about elementary number theory, then however compact the language our utterances in such cases will be infinitely long. If our utterances in such cases can be finite, then the corresponding gestalts will not contain all the available information, and we have seen that this cannot be.

Still, it is possible that I have done Delany an injustice in arguing that Babel-17 makes everything explicit. Let us set aside that problem. There remains another basic difficulty with the language. Wong teaches the Butcher to use "you" and "I." Since she does this in English, there is no immediate problem. We already have the words and the underlying concepts. But could you introduce these in Babel-17?

You could not. The whole language is built to express gestalts. The distinction between self and other would destroy the integral character of the gestalts; it is simply incompatible with the gestalt mode. Wong does refer to the augmented Babel-17 as Babel-18,[20] but if the gestalt mode were not modified in it, Babel-18 would be impossible. It must have a different structure.

Delany clearly is aware of the importance of the problems that he has treated, though they run deeper than he could pursue them in a work of fiction. Having pointed out his philosophical difficulties, I must admit that they don't bother me at all when I read the book. Besides, with a little tinkering, maybe I could get around them, and then? Well, no one here today could speak Babel-17, because the language as described is not possible. But tomorrow? That might be another story.

8.

Who Inhabits Riverworld?

MONTE COOK

Monte Cook's contributions to the combined study of science fiction and philosophy have earned him continued respect, and are reflected by his regularly appearing on the programs of the Science Fiction Research Association and the Popular Culture Association. He is also the only scholar to have two essays included in this book: "Tips for Time Travel" appears earlier.

Who inhabits Philip José Farmer's Riverworld?[1] At first blush, the answer is easy: aside from a few extraterrestrials, the inhabitants are men, women, and children from Earth. In fact, excluding imbeciles, idiots, and those who died before the age of five, every human being who died between 2,000,000 B.C. and 2008 A.D. lives there, a total of 36,006,009,637 persons. Farmer chronicles the adventures of only a few of these persons on Riverworld, but according to a note preceding *The Dark Design* even you and I are there. (Since not everyone now alive will be dead by 2008, how he knows that we are there is unclear; perhaps he is just playing the odds.)

The problem with this answer is the way that we all seem to have gotten to Riverworld. For one thing, we had to die first. And we didn't get there by spaceship, nor by somehow being beamed across space. In the first three volumes of the Riverworld series one gets the following picture of how we got from Earth to Riverworld: first the Ethicals— the beings in charge of Riverworld—somehow made recordings of every cell of every human being on Earth; then they played these recordings into energy-matter converters to reproduce the bodies of human beings as they were at the moment of death; next they rejuvenated these bodies and made new recordings of the rejuvenated bodies; and finally they destroyed the rejuvenated bodies and used the new recordings to materialize the bodies on the surface of Riverworld. (This process is also used for persons who die on Riverworld. Up-to-the-minute recordings are used to materialize their bodies again at a different place on the surface of Riverworld.)

The way that we got from Earth to Riverworld is problematic because our bodies on Riverworld are different from our bodies on Earth. There is no resurrection of the actual body of the person who died on Earth; the body on Riverworld is a duplicate of that body.

This raises the question of whether the person on Riverworld is the same person as the one who died on Earth or whether he too is a duplicate. True, the person called "Richard Burton" on Riverworld looks just like the nineteenth-century explorer Richard Burton looked at the age of twenty-five. And, though such things are not discussed in the Riverworld series, no doubt his fingerprints, voiceprints, and so forth, would match. Moreover, the Richard Burton of Riverworld has the personality of the actual (Earth) Richard Burton and seems to have all the memories that the actual Richard Burton would have. By any ordinary test, he *is* Richard Burton.

Still, the above picture of how the Richard Burton of Riverworld has been produced on the surface of Riverworld suggests that he is not the actual Richard Burton, but a duplicate. In fact, since the same process is used after deaths on Riverworld, it seems that there is not one but several Richard Burtons of Riverworld. If the process results not in the same person but in duplicates, then there is the Richard Burton of Earth, the first Richard Burton of Riverworld, and the 777 Richard Burtons after each death of a Richard Burton on Riverworld—a total of 779 Richard Burtons! (All the same, to simplify things I shall generally ignore the possibility that each death of Richard Burton on Riverworld results in a new person called "Richard Burton.")

The inhabitants of Riverworld will, of course, think that they are the same persons who died on Earth. When Peter Frigate suggests to his fellow Riverworlders Herman Göring and Richard Burton that the persons on Riverworld are not the same persons as were on Earth, they find the suggestion very disturbing. They feel threatened by the suggestion that they are just duplicates and that their memories are false memories.[2] (Though it is not mentioned, they perhaps feel threatened by the possibility that they are not even persons; it is far from clear that such duplicates would be persons.)

The inhabitants of Riverworld are not likely to change their minds. Not only will their psychologies resist the suggestion that they are duplicates, but practical considerations will make it natural for them to treat a person as if he were the same person who died on Earth.

Whether the inhabitants of Riverworld are duplicates or not, on Riverworld as on Earth, one would not want to take Lucrezia Borgia or King Henry VIII for a mate, trust one's country to Benedict Arnold, or pick a fight with Muhammad Ali. Moreover, as far as the inhabitants of Riverworld can determine, everything suggests their being the same persons who died on Earth and nothing points against it—except for the problem of how they got to Riverworld, and no one is very clear on how that happened. (If they were to run into other persons who looked just like them and had the same personality and memories, their confidence might be shaken; but that doesn't happen on Riverworld.)

Even if the inhabitants of Riverworld are duplicates, they will do just as well as the real things, so it may seem that it shouldn't matter whether or not they are duplicates. But it should matter to the inhabitants of Riverworld because many things depend upon the identification of the person on Riverworld with the person on Earth.

If we assume a retributive view of punishment, should the inhabitants of Riverworld punish Jack the Ripper upon finding out who he was? Should they praise Mozart for the music he wrote or blame Hitler for his atrocities? We know that the Sam Clemens on Riverworld feels guilty because he believes himself responsible for the death of his only son. No doubt he will feel guilty whether or not he is a duplicate, but should he feel guilty if he is not the Sam Clemens of Earth?

The question of whether or not the inhabitants of Riverworld are duplicates should matter to us because, remember, either we or our duplicates are on Riverworld. If *we* are on Riverworld, then we survive the death of our bodies. To understand why it should matter, consider the Riverworld series as future history and suppose that Farmer discusses "your" life on Riverworld in volume four of the series. And suppose that it turns out that both you and Sam Clemens are tortured. Should the one case of torture be more distressing than the other? Should you feel sympathy or terror for the "you" on Riverworld?

The problem with the earlier explanation of how Riverworlders got from Earth to Riverworld is that nothing seemed to move from one planet to the other. No part of the body on Earth ever left Earth. If this process of transportation from Earth to Riverworld were the whole story, then it would be difficult to avoid the conclusion that Riverworld is populated by duplicates. But it turns out not to be the whole story.

Several times in the first three volumes of the Riverworld series it is suggested that in addition to the body on Earth and its duplicate on Riverworld there is a soul or something analogous to one. In the fourth and final volume, *The Magic Labyrinth*, we are explicitly told that this soul—called the *wathan*—solves the problem of how a person on Riverworld can be identical with a person on Earth.[3] Now there is something that travels from Earth to Riverworld, and this passage seems to justify the idea that the Riverworlders are identical to the persons who died on earth.

Unlike the body, the *wathan* in not duplicated; it is brought from the dead body on Earth and attaches to the duplicate body on Riverworld. Thus there is a direct link between the person on Earth and the person on Riverworld.

The suggestion that a *wathan* travels from the person on Earth to the person on Riverworld focuses attention on the link between the two persons. Surely the right sort of link is what is required for Richard Burton of Riverworld and Richard Burton of Earth to be the same person. If Richard Burton had gotten from Earth to Riverworld by spaceship, then there would have been the right sort of link; and if Richard Burton of Riverworld had been made from scratch and just happened to look like and seem to have the memories of Richard Burton on Earth, then there would not have been the right sort of link. No amount of similarity between the Richard Burton of Riverworld and the Richard Burton of Earth, whether it is physical similarity or mental, can make them the same person.

Does the *wathan* offer a link that guarantees the identity of persons on Riverworld with their Earth counterparts? I want to consider first what seems to be a powerful objection to any such guarantee. The objection is that there is no connection between a soul or anything like it and our notion of someone being the same person. How could there be such a connection? We don't even know for sure that there is a soul; yet we can usually determine whether someone is the same person without any great difficulty. And we don't decide whether Smith is the same Smith that we met earlier by checking out his soul. We might reflect on whether he resembles the Smith that we met earlier or ask him whether he remembers meeting us.

If the soul did guarantee personal identity, then all our ordinary criteria for personal identity would be irrelevant. We should have to say of a person who looked, acted, and in every way seemed unlike Richard Nixon that he was Nixon if he had Nixon's soul; and surely this is counterintuitive.

Despite its considerable plausibility, this objection fails. To show that it fails, I am going to draw a parallel between the *wathan* and the brain. First I need to appeal to your intuitions about the role of the brain in personal identity.

Suppose that you and a friend are going to have an operation in which your brain is going to be put in his head and his brain in your head. Will the result be that you will each get a new body or that you will each get a new brain? If one body was going to be stretched on the rack, which would you prefer it to be?[4]

It seems to me and, I think, to most persons, that you will get a new body, not a new brain, and that unless you are a masochist you would want your old body to be put on the rack. (One undergraduate I asked wanted her friend's brain, and I am told that there is a Boris Karloff movie in which the mad doctor tries to save his friend's life by putting someone else's brain in his friend's body. I find both of these odd.)

Assuming that your intuitions agree with mine so far, I want to introduce a slight twist. Suppose now that your brain is going to be transplanted into a body that is an artificially made duplicate of your body and your body destroyed (perhaps your body has some sort of cancer). Will you survive the operation, now in a new body? Again it seems intuitive to me that you will have gotten a new body. This last case, of course, is getting close to the Riverworld case.

We can now see what is wrong with the objection that a physical soul could have nothing to do with personal identity. The difficulty, in short, is that the objection should equally show that the brain can have nothing to do with personal identity; and that, we have just seen, is not true. We can determine whether someone is the same person without even knowing that there is such a thing as a brain; and we can decide whether someone is the same person we met earlier without checking out his brain. But still, in the cases above, the brain determined the identity of the person.

One might counter my suggestion that the brain can determine the identity of a person by suggesting that it is not the brain but memories that do so. After all, we feel that the brain transplant will give us new bodies rather than new brains because we know (or suppose) that all our memories will go with our brains. Thus it is our memories that matter.

One response to this is to consider a case in which, after the brain transplant, the person with your brain has amnesia. Wouldn't you say that in this case you had developed amnesia and that you have a special interest in this person's not being tortured?

But a better response, because it is more enlightening, is to draw a contrast between memories and *seeming* memories. That a person *seems* to remember things, of course, doesn't mean that he *does* remember them. A person could, for example, be hypnotized into believing that he remembered certain things. Seeming memories surely don't guarantee personal identity. A person could even be hypnotized (or some other process could be used) so that he *seemed* to remember all the things that another person could *actually* remember. (In fact, this is one worry of the persons on Riverworld—are all of their Earth "memories" just seeming memories?)

For a person's memories to be genuine, the right sort of causal link must exist between his experiences and his memories of these experiences. Normally there is no problem about there being such a link: a person's experiences are recorded in his brain and can later be invoked by memory. But without the continuing presence of the brain to link present memories to past experiences, it is not clear how past experiences could affect present memories in the right sort of way.

The brain's role in establishing personal identity should now be a little clearer. The mere fact that a part of the body is connected to another body does not matter. If the arm of the Richard Burton on Earth were put on a spaceship, transported to Riverworld, and connected to the body of the Richard Burton of Riverworld, that would not make them the same person. But if this were done with the brain, they could naturally be taken to be the same person.

The crucial difference is that the brain plays a very important causal role. It is, as we saw, especially important to memory. If the Richard Burton on Riverworld remembers seeing something on Earth and his memory is genuine, then he must have seen that something on Earth and there must be the right sort of causal link between his seeing it then and his remembering it later on Riverworld. And the presence of the same brain on Riverworld as on Earth would make possible such a causal link.

But of course the brain doesn't travel from Earth to Riverworld; the *wathan* does. If in *The Magic Labyrinth* Farmer had treated the *wathan* as playing the role that we (mistakenly, it would turn out) attribute to the brain, he could have guaranteed the right sort of link between a person on Earth and a person on Riverworld in order for them to be the same person. He could have supposed that the *wathan* is the important part of us that provides the link between past experiences and present memories, determines our characters, and so on.

Instead, Farmer treats *wathans* as synthetically produced forms of "extraphysical energy" that, when attached to human zygotes, produce self-awareness in human beings and record everything necessary to duplicate their bodies.[5] Unfortunately, such entities fail to provide the right sort of link between a person on Earth and person on Riverworld. The mere fact that they record everything necessary to duplicate the body of a person on Earth does not guarantee that it is the same person on Riverworld, even if the recording itself is part of the person on Riverworld. To the extent that they are recordings, they are simply appendages that play no role in the life of the person.

They are not simply appendages, we are told, when it comes to a person's self-awareness—they are the source of that self-awareness. And it is this feature of *wathans*, not their role as recordings, that is supposed to guarantee the identity of Riverworlders with their Earth counterparts. Still, the fact that they stimulate self-awareness does not guarantee this identity, even if the same *wathan* stimulates self-awareness in an Earth person and then later in a person on Riverworld. A chemical that stimulated self-awareness would not guarantee such identity, even if the chemical were taken from a person on Earth and injected into a person on Riverworld (we can even imagine that the chemical somehow recorded the make-up of the body). Why should a form of "extraphysical energy" be any different?

At one point, we are told that the *wathan* is not just the source of self-awareness but also the "seat" of self-awareness and that when a *wathan* leaves a dead body it "takes its self-awareness with it."[6] It's not clear what this means, but the suggestion is that the *wathan* is the self. The *wathan* is the thing that has self-awareness, and if so, it must be the self. One thing wrong with this suggestion is that the *wathan* predates the self and thus can't be the self. But even ignoring this, we've been given at most what has the appearance of a solution to our problem. We have been told that the inhabitants of Riverworld are the persons who died on Earth, because the selves of those persons have travelled to Riverworld. Until we are told what a self is and how it can travel bodiless from Earth to Riverworld, such a solution is no solution at all.

I conclude then that the *wathan* can't do its job. The inhabitants of Riverworld are in the end not men, women, and children from Earth. Or, if one urges that it is after all up to the author of the Riverworld series whether they are or not, then they are men, women, and children from Earth—but how they got to Riverworld remains a mystery.

9.

Multiple Selves
and Survival of Brain Death

FRANK DILLEY

*Frank B. Dilley received his bachelors and masters
degrees in philosophy at Ohio University, a master of
divinity at Union Theological Seminary, and a doctorate
in philosophy at Columbia University. His primary area
of specialization is the philosophy of religion, in which
he has published seventeen articles in a wide variety of
journals, a book,* Metaphysics and Religious Language
*(New York: Columbia University Press, 1964), and
numerous reviews.*

*An earlier draft of the following essay was presented
at the August 1977 meeting of the American
Psychological Association. I later invited him to present
it at the Popular Culture Association Convention in
Pittsburgh in 1979. In it, Dilley considers the possibility
of life after death given a physicalistic understanding of
the self, especially regarding such an understanding as
it is represented in science fiction stories.*

*Dilley has been the chairman of two philosophy
departments: at Millikin University, from 1962 to 1967,
and at the University of Delaware, from 1967 to 1970 and
again from 1974 to the present. Between 1970 and 1974,
Dilley gave up the department chairmanship to be the*

university's associate provost. He has been a full
professor of philosophy since he arrived at Delaware in
1967.

Let us suppose, as physicalists do, that your self is a set of physical
states produced by electrochemical modifications of your brain substance. This view is not a strange one, and is probably held by most
science-minded people. The view is plausible because experiences really occur for us as a result of messages reaching our brains, and memories of those experiences are stored there.

Experiences occur in the physical world (and that for physicalists is
the only world, hence their name) as processes going on in the brain.
Physicalists used to think these processes took place in the heart but
now they feel the evidence points conclusively to the brain.

When you see something, what is going on in the physical world is a
process in your brain and nothing more; likewise when you store that
image and later remember it, both the storing and the recalling are
brain processes and nothing more. Memories consist of electrochemical modifications of brain cells.[1]

The contrasting view is usually known as mentalism or dualism.
Mentalists claim that although experiences of the outside world usually
or always reach us through the brain, our sensations occur in our
minds rather than in our brains. Mentalists feel that the self resides primarily or exclusively in the mind. They believe that physical memory
traces are stored in the brain, presumably making it possible for a person to acquire false memories by brain modification. But a mentalist assumes that if you switched her brain, she might wake up with false
memories and a false sense of who she is, but she would really be the
same person she was. Her self resides in her mind, which is something
separate from her brain. There is a ghost in the machine, and selves are
ghostly.

I will just assume for the sake of analysis that physicalism, in its bundle form, could provide grounding for our usual sense of self-identity
over time, and therefore for our usual sense of regarding our own future states as matters of personal concern. The question then is, assuming physicalism in its bundle form, could brain death possibly be sur-

vived? Since physicalists have no soul which could pass from one body to another, or from a body to a disembodied state, how could survival be possible?

If brain cells were immortal, this question would never even arise. But no one knows whether or not immortality is biologically feasible. If we could be made immortal then we would not have to "survive" death because death would not happen. The interesting question is, even if death is an inevitable biological fact, could we survive death through some sort of transplantation of ourselves from our original brains into something else? Many philosophers have said that such survival would not be possible based on any theory of self, but I want to argue that it is, based on every major theory of self. [2]

Survival of brain death should be possible based on both mentalist and physicalist views. In mentalist views the possibility can be expressed easily – the mind (or soul) merely transfers brains; but in physicalist views there seems to be no "something" to transfer since the physicalist conception of self says that the self just *is* its brain. Closer attention to what the physicalist theory really implies makes the possibility of self-transfer without brain-transfer plausible.

My self is a set of brain cells which are modified in particular ways. In the normal case the cells are modified through messages they receive from outside the brain (optic nerve, bloodstream, etc.), but there is no reason why the modifications could not in principle be produced by other than the normal means. Physicalists should therefore believe it possible in principle to produce my visual experiences directly in my brain by sending the brain the proper information.

Do I need eyes to see? The experience of seeing red occurs to my brain when a particular message ("red") reaches the proper brain center. Usually the message comes from the optic nerve, but actual eyes should not be required as long as a message identical to the one the optic nerve would have transmitted reaches the proper brain center.

Similarly, it should not matter whether the original cells which stored the memory message are the source of a subsequent memory message as long as the brain receives an identical message to the one the original cells would have sent.

Brain researchers now report that experiences can be recalled by direct electrical stimulation of the brain. These memories seem to be unusually vivid repetitions of past experiences. Producing experiences by direct stimulation should be possible in principle. Also, the possibility of producing memories from duplicate cells seems to create no difficulties. It should be easy then to think of the self surviving its original physical embodiment. There is no reason to think that duplicate systems should deliver anything different than what their originals delivered – the duplicate has everything the original did.

Suppose that a group of your brain cells is doomed because of some impending and irreversible failure in their ability to accept nutrients. A skillful surgeon saves the situation by recording the contents of those cells (both structural and electrical), removing them, and then adding fresh cells which are modified to exactly duplicate the originals. She then connects the new group of cells with the rest of the brain and wakes you.

Your computer has a new "memory," its original having been replaced by an exact duplicate. The duplicate should deliver the same messages that the original did, hence you should still "remember" what those original cells had stored. The presence of the memories should be independent of whether original or duplicate cells deliver them to your brain. It should make no difference whether the cells are replaced a few at a time or all at once (by inserting a suitably modified fresh brain); your memories and responses should still be there. You would have survived the death of your brain cells through duplication.

If this much be granted, survival of brain cell death can be extended even further. The needed modifications could be stored as specifications for the subsequent creation of a new brain (or new cells for an old brain). Our present selves do not exist strictly uninterrupted; self-identity transcends the gaps in our consciousness we call sleep and comas, so even long storage should cause no particular problem.

A physicalistic theory of the self should lead us to conclude, then, that the nature of the self is not altered even if all its parts have been replaced, and even if the replacement set is started up much later in time.

The possibility of self-transplants can be reinforced by another example. Let us suppose that memory switching is possible, as it should be if physicalism is true. Suppose that Jo's brain is erased and Meg's pattern is recorded on Jo's brain. Jo's brain now has been modified so that its states are duplicates of the states originally contained in Meg's brain. We wake the person who used to be Jo and ask her who she is.

I think we would all expect her to say that she is Meg, not that she is Jo. The reason we expect this is that all of her memories and responses would be Meg-memories and Meg-responses, not Jo-memories and Jo-responses. It would be difficult to say that although she thinks she is Meg she is really Jo. After all, in physicalism, what is a self except brain contents?

An analogy can provide additional reinforcement, yet it points beyond to some problems we need to examine. A tune is the same even when played on different records. It can be imprinted on many pieces of matter at once without destroying its identity as a tune. Imagine that you stroll past a series of speakers, each connected with a copy of the same master record. You recognize the tune as the same: it's "Old Black Joe." Suppose you met several copies of the now aging Josephine Premice and that you talked to each of them about her identity. Would you be willing to say of each of them, it's "Old Black Jo"?

If a self, physically considered, is a set of electrochemical states, organized in a particular pattern, it should make no difference to selfhood whether the pattern is imprinted once or a hundred times. Each imprint would be that self. The philosopher Nietzsche recognized the validity of this claim and called it "eternal recurrence."

But the very possibility of multiple selves makes the notion of self-transfer problematic. Doesn't it seem wrong to claim that many numerically different people could have the same self? The same tune can be played on many records and, if the analogy is good, so could several coexisting bodies have the same selves.

Further, suppose that our surgeon kept the old cells after she removed them and then reassembled them. Having all the original components of the brain, she puts them back together again and starts up the original brain in a fresh body. Do we now have a self and its duplicate or do we have two instances of the same self? Suppose we kept Meg intact while recording Meg-memories on Jo's brain, do we have two Megs now, one in Meg's body and one in Jo's?

Moreover, once we have two Meg selves, can they really be the same self? Beginning at that point in time they no longer have the same subsequent experiences and therefore become increasingly different. It is difficult to imagine two selves as being the same and yet numerically different. And how could they become increasingly different while remaining the same? It defies common sense.

In the following section, two science fictional accounts of personality duplication will be presented. Then an attempt will be made to clarify the apparent contradiction that duplicate selves are the same as the self they duplicate, but not the same as each other once duplication has occurred. My analysis proceeds from physicalist and bundle theory assumptions. I have avoided clone models because they would not work — my clones would closely resemble me but would not have undergone my personal modifications.

THE EXAMPLES

Frederick Pohl and Jack Williamson have explored person duplication in their novel *The Farthest Star*, (New York: Ballantine Books, 1975). Tachyon transmission has been discovered, and because the lower limit of the speed of tachyons is that of light, tachyon transmission has made rapid space travel feasible. Every atom and molecule in a person is scanned, all positions and relationships among those atoms are recorded, and the resultant information is transmitted by a tachyon beam to a receiver. A duplicate person is assembled at the receiving point.

The original person, Pohl and Williamson suppose, is unharmed by the process and, as they describe it, "the man who volunteered for a tachyon trip stayed at home. What flashed across space was a description of himself, and what emerged from the receiving chamber at destination was a new-built identical copy. There was no detectable difference between original and copy."

As would be expected, persons who become related in specific ways to duplicate selves have the same relationships to the duplicates as they have with the originals; duplicated selves feel the same toward other people as their originals do. Zara expresses grave concern because the duplicate of her husband Ben Pertin will die in remote space while being fully aware that the original husband was still at home. The duplicate Pertin bitterly laments the fact that he was not present with the wife that he loved. He has the same feeling toward Zara that his original had, and regards himself fully as the Ben who loves Zara.

When asked about her concern for his duplicate, Zara says to Ben, "I love you, and he is you, and I don't like to think about what is happening to him." For her there are now two Ben Pertins, one at home and one far away. The duplicated self expresses his feelings this way:

> So, on Sun One, one Ben Pertin had walked out of the chamber, in no way different than when he had gone in. He had done whatever he had to do in the balance of that working day, and at the end of it returned again to Zara, his/their wife. But on the wheel, another Ben Pertin had floated out of the receiving chamber and had felt the instant shock of knowing that he had lost the gamble. He was the one on the wheel.

The duplicate Ben laments further that between the selves there is only one real difference — one is still at home, the other is far away.

Of course duplication can have its complications. For example, a Pertin duplicate eventually meets and of course immediately loves a Zara duplicate. The complication occurs because this duplicate Zara had come from a version of Zara which preceded the one Pertin had met and married. To the Pertin duplicate, Zara is a duplicate of the self he married; to the duplicate of the pre-Pertin Zara, he is an absolute unknown. In fact, he never wins this Zara's affections on "The Farthest Star."

The duplicates behave just as would be anticipated from the theory outlined earlier. Each duplicate regards itself as the same self as the original even though after duplication each has a separate center of consciousness and has different subsequent experiences. Outsiders react to the duplicates as though they were the originals and the duplicates have exactly the same feelings toward outsiders as the originals had.

All this conforms to expectations because although each duplicated self has a separate consciousness, each is related by duplication to the same set of internal states as the original, and retains that set in its own past. The identity of a self is determined by its contents, and each duplicate had the "same" contents, and so is the "same" self as the one it duplicated.

The idea of survival through self-transplants used by Robert Silverberg in *To Live Again* (New York: Dell Publishing Company, 1969) is more complex and perhaps more problematical because of the difficulty in conceiving just how two selves can use the same brain.[3] Silverberg supposes a state of technology less advanced than that in "The Farthest Star." The possibilities of self-duplication have not been perfected, but techniques of brain-scanning and brain-recording have.

Through the development of the Scheffing process (named but not thoroughly described) a person may have a self recording made. Old recordings are periodically replaced by updates, and the old version supposedly destroyed. The reason for updating is that when the self recording is eventually imprinted as a secondary self in some other body, the "persona" will be the most completely developed version of that self that it has been feasible to maintain.

The person who wishes to acquire a persona requests an appropriate one from the library. After suitable checking for compatibility, a new persona can be granted. The instructions given those undergoing the Scheffing process promise them "complete access to the memories and life experiences of the imprinted persons," warn of some possible confusion of identities for a short while, and urge that the new persona be regarded as a guest and partner. The relationship with that persona is the most intimate personal relationship possible.

What happens from the point of view of the original person, Silverberg says, is that a secondary self has been acquired. Because the new persona shares the nervous system of the host, from the persona's point of view it is reincarnated. This can become a complete reincarnation if it should happen that the persona takes over the body of the host, "goes dybbuk." Naturally, precautions are taken to introduce a persona only when the host is deemed strong enough to dominate that second self. Takeovers are discouraged by a rule that calls for their erasure should they be detected.

DISCUSSION

It is easy to see why duplicates might regard themselves as successors to their originals. After all, they have the same sense of self and all the memories of their predecessors. It seems easy to accept the idea of self-duplication thus far. So long as a self is a bundle of experiences which includes some other bundle, it includes that self. How can we balk at the idea that successor selves should be regarded as continuations of their predecessors?

It would seem arbitrary to do so. After all, the relation of my present self to my past selves, on the physicalist bundle model, is merely that of inclusion. I am the "same" self I was yesterday because my present bundle of experiences includes my past bundle. Personas have the same right to call themselves "me" as my own future states, if the required relation is merely inclusion. In any case, Silverbergian characters regard their future selves as themselves reincarnated, and the reincarnated personas regard themselves as reincarnations of their former selves.[4]

But what would be the relationship between two copies of the same recorded persona? As far as I can tell, Silverberg does not deal with that eventuality in *To Live Again*. But the Pohl and Williamson story does consider that possibility and treats it as would be expected. Though each successor self incarnates its predecessor, no successor self regards another simultaneously existing duplicate as the same as itself. Duplication involves the existence of one self at one moment in time and two or more selves which are continuations of it at a later moment in time; but the two later selves are not really the same as each other, they are merely equal successors of their preduplicate stage.

In *The Farthest Star*, the selves who are duplicated do not regard their duplicates as really themselves, but as continuations of their preduplicated selves. Ben, as he dies, takes comfort in the fact that elsewhere in the universe he lives on through his duplicate. Once duplicates are created, the course of each life affects only that copy, so to duplicates it seems immaterial what subsequently happens to the others. Is that attitude incorrect?

I suggest that it is not. We are not compelled to choose between the two novels because both are correct in their attitudes, as I will try to

show. A duplicated self is the continuation of the self which it duplicated, but from that point on each has a separate history, hence has no
"existential" concerns with what happens to its duplicates. This should
clear up the conflict between two sets of seemingly correct intuitions
with which this discussion of science fiction illustrations was preceded.[5]

Let us grant that any self has its present personal identity because of
the set of experiences which it embodies. All Ben's duplicates will say
when awakened, "My name is Ben," and they will each love Zara and
all Zara duplicates. Each has the proper memories imbedded in the
proper place in its memory set and will respond to those memories in
the way Ben characteristically does. The character, value structure,
and patterns of thinking will all be Ben's, and anyone who knows Ben
recognizes the duplicates as Ben. Different types of bodies might introduce an identification problem for external observers, but not for the
Bens themselves, who could identify themselves immediately by their
memories.

However, each duplicate will have a different future life history from
the moment of awakening, much as my present self has a different future life history from my own past self. My past self had none of the future awarenesses that my present self has had, and yet it seems perfectly normal to say that I am the continuation of my own past self
nonetheless. I would still regard my own future self as me despite the
fact that I (my present self) will not have its subsequent experiences. If
that is true then I should not have qualms about regarding later duplicates as me.

The illusion of contradiction vanishes once the claims are stated
clearly. My future self (selves) is (are) continuous with my past self;
therefore I am existentially concerned with it (them). But this does not
imply that each of my duplicates will have existential concerns about
each other.

The selves were previously one, hence the preduplicated single self is
existentially concerned with all of them. But the duplicated selves are
now numerous and have no existential concern with each other. Each
duplicated self is concerned only about its present and future states and

not anyone else's. Once duplicate selves exist, they are externally related to each other's present experience, internally related only to their own.

In short, the persona implanted by the Scheffing process is a continuation of the self which awaited transplant in just the same sense as my future selves are continuations of my present self. Any past Ben or Zara should regard its duplicates as continuations or incarnations, and should regard itself as being multiplied by the process, though each duplicate will have a separate life history from that point on. Duplicates will share no experiences with each other and therefore will have no concern with each other.

On the one hand there are good arguments for saying that if the self is a bundle of brain states related in a certain way, then wherever that combination exists that self exists. On the other hand a doubt was raised, based on the argument that multiple copies are not the same self since their centers of awareness are different and since subsequent experience for each would not constitute states of awareness for the original and so could not sustain that original self.

I have argued that there is really no conflict in saying that the selves are continuations of the same self when duplicated and that they are no longer the same selves after duplication. Mentalists believe in "the ghost in the machine"—that when you strip all the contents from the self, you still have left over the owner of those contents. But physicalists believe that the self is just its bundle of perceptions and memories and nothing over and above that bundle.

What constitutes your self's continuity during periods of sleep and comas? When the sleep switch is thrown normal consciousness vanishes. When it is thrown again, your self springs back to life. Selves transcend gaps in time; or rather we should say, whenever the self is turned on it is there and whenever it is turned off it is not there. It is the activation of the set of states that constitutes the self and nothing more.

As physicalists we do not have to reject either intuition. Duplication of brain contents constitutes duplication of self. But when two duplicates exist they are mere continuations of the same selves, each having a separate self-awareness. Each of the two includes the preduplicated original but not each other. Once they are two, each has its own subsequent future history, hence what happens to one does not happen to the other.

Ben may have sympathy for his duplicates as I have sympathy for my brother, but each Ben does not experience the inner states of his duplicates any more than I experience those of my brother. In physicalism one predecessor can have two or more successors, although that would be nonsense in mentalism. The descriptions of Ben and Zara are philosophically sound.

Only mentalists should find duplicate selves paradoxical, for reasons I have mentioned. Mentalists have no room in their theories for self-duplication since they believe the self is the owner of the bundle and not the bundle itself. No mentalist would go into the tachyon transmitter. In fact neither the Silverberg model or the Pohl and Williamson model would work for mentalists.

Of course, as has been said repeatedly, if physicalism cannot give an adequate grounding for our sense of self-identity, we are forced to make a choice. The two science fiction models give us all the sense of self-identity and survival of brain death that a bundle theory could give us. If it takes mentalism to give us the sense of self-identity we think we have, so much for the adequacy of our sense of self-identity—or for physicalism.

10.

The Coalescence of Minds

STAN MC DANIEL

*Stan McDaniel received his bachelors degree in
philosophy from the University of California, Santa
Barbara, and his masters in philosophy from the
University of California, Los Angeles. He has taught at
the California State University, Sonoma, since 1966.*

*McDaniel's relationship with science fiction goes
back to the early 1940s, when he contributed regularly
to the letter columns of science fiction magazines.
Since that time he has continued this relationship in a
variety of ways: his musical compositions were
performed at the first and second OCTOCON Science
Fiction Conventions in Santa Rosa, California, in
October of 1977 and 1978, and he is now at work on a
major work of fantasy entitled* The Saga of Stoneglow
Threescar. *McDaniel has also written and published
work on Nietzsche (including a book of that name with
Thor Publications) and philosophical percept theory.*

*The following essay concerns the possibility of
group-minds. Though critical of typical SF treatments
of this concept which employ telepathy, McDaniel*

117

*thinks that science fiction also provides at least one
other, in this case philosophically coherent, model for
such entities.*

Among the concepts which appear in science fiction and which have philosophical interest is that of group-mind.

A group-mind, very roughly speaking, is a *coalescence of minds:* a single mind formed by means of a special connection between the minds of several physically distinct individuals. The bond between the individuals must be a far stronger one than that afforded by ordinary communication. Telepathy is universally adopted in science fiction as the mode of connection between minds which makes group-mind possible.

This dependence upon the concept of telepathy seriously weakens the concept of group-mind, because the concept of telepathy is one of the weakest philosophically in science fiction. A widely accepted set of ideas about telepathy exists in science fiction literature; the ideas are inconsistent with one another but are regularly invoked as though they formed a consistent whole. Science fiction stories vacillate between physicalistic and dualistic interpretations of telepathy; in the long run, the physicalistic view becomes secondary. Telepathy, as it is employed in science fiction, is a notion which trades upon the metaphysics of mind-body dualism.

There is not sufficient space in this paper to detail the difficulties found in such a view of telepathy. In my opinion, careful analysis shows that the concept is entirely inadequate. The purpose of this paper is not to support this particular point, but to explore what remains of the concept of group-mind after its supposed telepathic basis is discounted.

Parallel to the dualistic-telepathic concept of group-mind there can be discerned in science fiction hints of a quite different theoretical structure. This latter is generally overshadowed by the emphasis upon telepathy; however, I find it much the more interesting side of the group-mind concept.

Most group-mind stories, for instance, suggest that the appearance of group-mind is a function of the dynamics of evolution. Within the evolutionary framework, the transition from individual minds to group-mind is depicted as a qualitative change of the sort that has come to be called *synergistic:* The post-threshold state is not analyzable in pre-threshold terms, and is marked by an increase in energy associated with new properties.

In Arthur C. Clarke's well-known group-mind novel, *Childhood's End*, we find the following comment about the newly formed group-mind. Made up of the (disembodied) minds of the last generation of children on the Earth, it is about to leave the Earth to seek out its own special destiny—absorption by a galactic entity called the Overmind. The speaker is an alien observer, explaining the situation to an earthling of the older generation:

> All the earlier changes your race has known took countless ages. But this is a transformation of the mind, not of the body. By the standards of evolution, it will be cataclysmic—instantaneous. You must face the fact that yours is the last generation of Homo Sapiens. As to the nature of the change . . . we do not know how it is produced . . . what trigger impulse the Overmind employs when the time is ripe. All we have discovered is that it starts with a single individual . . . and then spreads explosively, like the formation of crystals around the first nucleus in a saturated solution. In a few years, it will all be over. . . . There is no future for the world you know. All the hopes and dreams of your race are ended now. You have given birth to your successors, and it is your tragedy that you will never understand them . . . will never even be able to communicate with their minds. Indeed, they will not possess minds as you know them. They will be a single entity, as you yourselves are the sums of your myriad cells.[1]

Here is the idea of synergistic transformation coupled with an evolutionary context. The specifics of the evolutionary theory are not clear; the passage contains a mixture of suggestions—mutation, interference—but also long preparation until "the time is ripe."

However, Clarke significantly uses the analogy of the supersaturated solution, an analogy which frequently arises in discussions of the problem of qualitative change along a continuum of development. For example, the philosopher-paleontologist, Pierre Teilhard, speaking of cellular evolution, says:

> We can assume that, though they only occurred in the first instance at a single point or a small number of points, the first cells multiplied almost instantaneously—as crystallization spreads in a super-saturated solution.[2]

This striking resemblance between Clarke's comment and Teilhard's serves to note that the account of evolution adopted in most science fiction is essentially the same as the theory of orthogenetic evolution which was advocated by Teilhard. Upon that theory, evolution proceeds by synergistic "leaps" along a continuum of development; and the orthogenetic theory of the Teilhardian type has the potential to account for group-mind without depending upon a prior commitment to telepathy as a necessary condition. I will attempt to sketch briefly the way in which the orthogenetic theory applies to the concept of group-mind, and how science fiction has used the orthogenetic theory.

"Orthogenetic" here indicates "having a definite orientation which offsets the effect of chance in the play of heredity."[3] According to Teilhard, the orientation of the evolutionary axis of development can be empirically determined. The evidence indicates, he held, that the orthogenesis is toward "increasing degrees of centro-complexity." He explains this as follows: "*The more complex a being is, the more it is centered upon itself and therefore the more conscious does it become.*"[4]

This idea of centro-complexity appears in the classic group-mind novel by the British philosopher and novelist, Olaf Stapledon. In this work, *Last and First Men* (1931), Stapledon wrote:

> The more complex the form, the more percipient and active the spirit. . . . There has been a long and fluctuating adventure toward harmonious complexity of form, and toward the awakening of the spirit into unity, knowledge, delight, and self-expression.[5]

Group-mind enters as a stage of development more complex than the stage of individual mind. It is correspondingly more "conscious," consciousness being the specific synergistic change of quality attendant upon increased complexity. The theory must be able to define "complexity" in such a way that it will be applicable to both individual mind and group-mind, and will allow for the ordering of these along a developmental continuum.

If the orthogenetic theory is combined with a theory of mind-brain identity (as it is in much of science fiction), this will be difficult to achieve. Evolutionary advance will be identified with a more convoluted, heavier, or larger brain. A group-mind becomes difficult to account for unless in some way a group of persons might share a single physical brain.

Stapledon's view in *Last and First Men* is mixed on this issue. Up to a certain point, he identifies evolutionary advance with increased brain size; when the biological limit of brain growth is reached, he postulates a group-mind. He attempts to give this group-mind a single physical brain, in a sense, by postulating a physical link between the individual brains of the group in the form of a "system of radiation," creating a kind of "superbrain." He calls this system "telepathic."

But this does not really answer the issue of complexity, and Stapledon seems to have recognized that. He asserts that the "telepathic" connection between the brains does not constitute their relationship as a group-mind, but merely forms a necessary physical basis for that relationship. As the novel continues, Stapledon makes it clear that the relationship between individuals which constitutes them as a group-mind is rather a particular *mode of association* between them.

This view, which defines increased complexity as a change in organizational quality, is one which John Dewey utilized in discussing the relationship between mind and language. Dewey employed an orthogenetic theory of evolution in connection with the mind-body question. He argued that the distinction between body and mind is not an absolute metaphysical one, but rather "one of increasing levels of complexity and intimacy of interaction." Mind, in this view, is "an added property assumed by a feeling creature when it reaches that organized interaction with other living creatures which is language."[6]

According to this approach, the locus of mind is not the brain, but the interacting social group. Grouping of individuals is the essential biological fact. Thus mind consciousness is already an early type of group consciousness. The problem of increasing intimacy of relationship (to the point of synergistic change), which science fiction regularly attempts to solve by an *ad hoc* introduction of telepathy, here takes on a different light.

The science fiction author ordinarily presupposes "minds" on a dualistic model, then treats the problem of increasing intimacy as one of bringing the minds "closer together" by *removing* language, which is looked upon as a barrier to direct communication.[7] But the Deweyan view identifies increasingly intimate modes of association with the *development of mind itself*—language being a necessary condition for such association. Language is not seen as a conversion of "nonphysical" thought into "physical" speech. The perfection of communication involves the perfection of language, not its removal.

Paradoxically, then, science fiction commonly accepts in basic outline the orthogenetic theory of evolution and places group-mind within that evolutionary context, yet maintains at the same time a dualistic-telepathic view, without recognizing these fundamental differences between the theories. The concept of group-mind generated by the orthogenetic theory is markedly different from that based upon dualistic assumptions. The focus moves from telepathy to centro-complexity.

The idea of centro-complexity is not a simple one. In the passage from *Childhood's End* just mentioned, Clarke says of the group-mind that it "will be a single entity, as you yourselves are the sums of your myriad cells." This comment addresses the question of centro-complexity by asserting an analogy between cellular complexity in relation to the organism, and mind-to-mind complexity in relation to the group. The unanswered question is: How exactly are we the "sums" of our "parts" (cells, organs, biological functions)?

Dewey approached this question in the following manner:

> The organism is not just a structure; it is a characteristic way of interactivity which is not simultaneous, but serial . . . each "part" of an organism is itself organized, and so of the "parts" of the part. Hence its selective bias in interactions with environing things is exercised so as to maintain itself, while also maintaining the whole of which it is a mem-

ber. This pervasive operative presence of the whole in the part and the part in the whole constitutes . . . the capacity of feeling.[8]

Here Dewey applies the idea of centro-complexity. "Feeling" is the consciousness-correlate (the synergistic result) of the mutual interplay of "parts" (the complexity). The concept of *functionality* has always appeared to me to be the primitive concept which underlies any such viewpoint; hence I call this type of complexity *functional differentiation*, and refer in general to the "parts" of the organic system as *functions*. Given this, it is possible to formulate a very general definition of group-mind, from an orthogenetic centro-complex standpoint, as follows:

> A group-mind is a temporal association of individual personalities such that the individuals are functionally differentiated to the degree where the synergistic result of their association is itself a personality.

This view does not depend upon telepathy at all. The type of association referred to is association in action through time, not association through telepathic conversation. Elements of this view do appear in science fiction. In E. E. Smith's group-mind novel, *Children of the Lens*, there are several instances, although officially Smith adopts the dualistic-telepathic explanation of group-mind. In describing the mode of action of the newly formed group-mind (called "the Unit"), for example, Smith writes:

> Everything happened at once. Karen's impenetrable block flared into being—not instantly, but instantaneously. Constance assembled and hurled, in the same lack of time, a mental bolt of whose size and power she had never been capable. Camilla, the detector-scanner, synchronized with the attacking thought and steered. And Kathryn and Kit, with all the force . . . of human heredity, got behind it and pushed. Nor was this, any of it, conscious individual effort. The Children of the Lens were not now five, but one. This was the Unit at work . . . no time whatever was lost in consultation or decision. Action was . . . simultaneous with perception.[9]

Here there is no question of private telepathic signalling by means of thought waves, which Smith elsewhere takes as the basis of group-mind. Instead we see spontaneous functional differentiation, similar to teamwork but differing in degree. The action of the individuals is coordinated not by plan, but by the systemic nature of the Unit itself—coordinated, that is, to a degree equivalent to the degree of organization existing among the functions of an individual human personality.

This type of spontaneous functional differentiation relative to a group-center is also the basis for the group-mind in Stapledon's *Last and First Men*. The group-minds of the Last Men (Eighteenth Race) are made up of ninety-six individuals, each of whom differs from the others in "temperament." This difference in temperament is essential to the group-mind, which is constituted by the special form of "harmonious activity" which blends the temperaments into a "group-self."

Stapledon says of the group-self that it would not be possible "did not the temperament and capacity of each [member] differ appropriately from those of the others." The temperaments themselves are not described, but are said to be analogous to our own differing psychological types "but with far greater range and diversity."[10]

Stapledon also called the different temperaments "sub-sexes," thinking of them as ramifications or refinements of our basic bisexuality.[11] Some connection between sexual dynamics and the dynamics of group-mind has regularly been suggested in science fiction. What has not been recognized is that this factor is not appropriate to the dualistic-telepathic model (in which "pure mind" must be kept separate from physical functions), but belongs properly to the orthogenetic theory (where continuity between physical, psychological, and intellectual differentiation must be maintained).

Teilhard, who was eminently concerned with eliminating the mind-body dichotomy, insisted that any adequate theory of the evolution of mind had to take sexuality into account in a fundamental way. He took group-mind to be an expression of human love—to be exact, he felt it was the perfection of human love.[12] This conclusion was in keeping with his orthogenetic model. In his "orthogenetic time" the future is necessarily *perfecting of the past*, this being the specific relation which the more-complex bears to the less-complex along the evolutionary axis.

I call this relation, which is an essential component of the orthogenetic (Teilhardian) model, the *perfecting relation*. Teilhard employed it in a religious manner by asserting that the achievement of group-mind by humanity as a whole was the equivalent, from the theological standpoint, of redemption — not just redemption of the human group, but of the entire evolutionary past.[13]

In science fiction the perfecting relation appears in connection with group-mind. Stapledon adopts it explicitly as "the liberation of the past" which becomes one of the chief purposes of the advanced races of mankind.[14]

In Smith's *Children of the Lens,* the perfecting relation appears as the specific duty of the group-mind toward the galactic civilization from which it has developed — the group-mind's task is to transform and uplift the moral order of the galaxy.

Other science fiction stories about group-mind employ the perfecting relation in varying ways and to varying degrees. Robert Heinlein's *Stranger in a Strange Land* suggests that group-mind entails an overall sexual and social liberation. It is almost universal, in such stories, that the group-mind is developed for the sake of bettering what came before it.

Clarke's *Childhood's End* is an exception to this. There the group-mind's action is not continuous with or responsible to the past. Instead, Clarke portrays a brutal severance: the group entity obliterates its own home planet and all of its forebears. This is one of the ways in which Clarke's story rejects the orthogenetic model, although in other respects it invokes that model.

Science fiction accounts of group-mind, then, intermix dualistic and nondualistic materials, with an obscuring effect: there is a tendency to shift from one view to the other at important points. Sometimes, the nondualistic (orthogenetic) material is offered as a "scientific explanation" of the otherwise dualistically conceived group-mind. But in fact the two lines of thought are logically separate and are not explanatory of one another.

In my opinion, the dualistic-telepathic aspect of science fiction stories detracts from the ideal of science fiction as a literature of scientific extrapolation. To the extent, however, that science fiction suggests the possibility of group-mind based upon orthogenetic centro-complexity, it does engage in productive extrapolation.

In conclusion, group-mind as defined above may be a genuine empirical possibility. The development of group-mind would lend confirmation to the orthogenetic theory which predicts it and would have profound implications for our view of the psychology of the person. But if the possibility of group-mind is to have the status of a scientific hypothesis, a more adequate concept of centro-complexity than that given in science fiction (or by Teilhard) must be supplied.

The needed explication of centro-complexity may be available by application of current nondualistic theories of mind and communication. In this paper, I have suggested how Dewey's approach (which is similar to that of Wittgenstein) may be helpful. Given a proper explication of centro-complexity, an experimental basis for the development of group-mind could be forthcoming. Readers of science fiction would surely welcome a true coalescence of minds, but they might have trouble recognizing one at first: its internal dynamics, as well as its outward behavior, would be far more subtle than the naive dualistic view telepathy allows.

11.

The Elusive Self and the Intimidating Other

ROBERT E. MYERS

Robert E. Myers received his doctorate at Ohio State University and has published a number of philosophical essays in a variety of journals. His experience with science fiction is extensive. He has done work in this area for both the American Culture Association and the Science Fiction Research Association. He also prepared a primary and secondary bibliography for the work of Jack Williamson. Williamson's own collection, Teaching Science Fiction: Education for Tomorrow, *will include one of Myers' essays: "Philosophic Insight Through Science Fiction: Focusing on Human Issues."*

The following essay considers the problems involved with concepts of the self and the other. Myers shows that science fiction can assist us in avoiding problematic solutions that nonetheless have had wide support in philosophical circles.

Myers is a professor of philosophy and department head at Bethany College in West Virginia.

The notions of "self" and "other" figure significantly in our lives. Reference to self and to other(s) and the recognition of a distinction between the two (whether the other be a person or thing), constitute ba-

sic components of our language, our thinking, reasoning, and emotional processes, our moral systems, as well as our societal, political,
and economic structures and even our social and individual identities.

However, we seem to be strangely unsure about how to use the two
terms as categories, especially since such terms and categories permeate
our lives and life activities. We are unsure about what the related concepts mean, about what we think (and feel) about such entities, and
about how we know them, if we can know them.

I will use three science fiction stories, one each by Asimov, Williamson, and Le Guin, (1) to indicate the nature and the range of the problem of self and other, (2) to highlight portions of this problem, and (3)
to illustrate the fundamental inadequacies of two popular solutions,
the Behavioral-Mechanical model and the Inner-Self Discovery model.
I will conclude with the suggestion that a more satisfactory solution
should include a balance of those aspects which these two widely accepted solutions either distort or ignore.

NATURE AND RANGE OF THE PROBLEM AREA

First, by way of introduction, consider "common sense." Common
sense is not concerned with explicating concepts, with explicit or implicit coherence, or the presence of contradictions. And yet upon this
uncritical collage of notions, ideas, and feelings, most people build beliefs and make decisions.

Common sense allows us to accept the following statements as obvious and true: A human being is a person. Machines are not persons. A
human being is different from a machine. I am a person; I am conscious; I perceive, think, and have a self-identity. You are different
from me, but I know you almost as well as I know myself, for you are a
person, too. Human beings, persons like me, have feelings, emotions,
wills, minds that think and reason, and maybe a soul. Human beings
can make choices, learn, and be creative. Machines are not like human
beings, for machines don't have these qualities and can't do these
things. I like machines, for I enjoy the benefits they provide. But at the

same time, I'm not sure that I do like machines—I identify very strongly with my job, with my work, but now I might be "replaced by a machine" which, I'm told, can perform better and at less cost work that I thought only human beings could do. Maybe it is true that some of the new, more complicated machines can "think," "reason" and "sense." I like having other human beings around, for I believe society provides me and my family with certain benefits. But at the same time, I'm not sure that I do like having others around, at least not too many of them and not all the time—you don't seem able to "get away" anymore; there's always a crowd wherever you go.

You know, when you get right down to it, other people—society—restrict me, invade my space and my personal rights, make demands on me and influence me and my kids in ways I'm not sure are right. It's important to be an individual and others keep me from realizing my individualism, from fully realizing my "self."

Here we see that few distinctions are more firmly established in Western languages and few categories are more persistent in the socio-political structures as well as in the "common sense" of the West, than are those of self and other. It seems that Western languages and category schemata do include and were intended to recognize the self and the other (that is, the "I" and the "Not-I"). Certainly we have recognized these categories in most of the areas of specialized study of society and individual—in the sociological, political, religious, educational, psychological, philosophical areas, and others. In each of these areas, the other seems presupposed in order to distinguish the self or person, and/or the self is presupposed to distinguish what is not-self or other. Especially interesting are certain subareas of economic and psychological orientation in which the other is seen as required for sales and service or as that to which we must "adjust," and the self is seen as the focal point of illness and health. Consider such terms as loss of self-identity, split or multiple selves, loss of contact with reality, the self intimidated by others or the well-adjusted self, the socially integrated self—all may be seen as somehow having economic as well as psychological relevance.

Admittedly, these terms or categories, explicitly or as presuppositions, pervade our linguistic and cultural experience, and they are used in a great number of ways. However, from these facts it does not follow (and it has not followed) that we clearly understand the meanings or the full significance of these concepts for our lives. On the contrary, it seems increasingly apparent that we are by no means certain as to what, if any, criteria are appropriate for making such distinctions, or for placing different "things" in one or the other of these categories.

The confusion resident in the uncritical level of common sense may reflect the confusion to be found at more critical levels. Perhaps many of the contemporary social and individual crises which we experience regularly—"crises" which someone identifies, which are then pursued frantically, but which finally, in futility, are left unresolved—result significantly from our frustrating inability to focus clearly on the meanings and referents of these basic but elusive concepts, that is, from the irresolution of what philosophers call "the problem of the self" and its correlate, "the problem of others."[1]

Two Popular Solutions and Their Inadequacies

Two temptingly simple, seemingly exclusive, proposed "solutions" of the self-other problem that are widely influential in modern society are what I will call (1) the Operational-Behavioral/Functional-Mechanical mode and (2) the Inner-Self Discovery model. Although each of these solutions has significant appeal and support, both seem, in different ways, to undercut the basis for making the self-other distinction and for continuing to use these categories in any usual sense, if at all.

In effect, the first model "solves" the problem by holding that no such elusive entity as the traditional self is required to understand what someone does, that public behavior(s) or operations are adequate to explain all such "things," whether we call them "me" or "you" or something else. Behavior is open to inspection by an observer—is observable—and can be changed by the proper systematic process of positive rewards.[2]

This process is often perceived—correctly or incorrectly—as being closely related to, or identical with, a form of mechanical model in which the human body is understood as a kind of machine or as a machinelike structure subject to intermediate control by a servo-mechanism, the brain. Fairly common in contemporary thought, this is a form of reductionism, the tendency to reduce a problem or a complex to one of its aspects and explain the existence (or nonexistence) of the other aspects as explicable in terms of the single aspect (or as not needed, since the single aspect alone is real—or capable of being dealt with by the explanatory model which has been adopted).[3]

The second widely influential "solution" in our contemporary setting is an attempt to solve the problem by retreating from it, by "turning within" to "discover the true self," to "fully actualize the self," to develop a total underlying *self*-sufficiency. This solution ignores the other and the basic social relationship of self and other—particularly things and persons, but not some mystical other—is seen either as inessential or as too threatening, too intimidating to the self to even try to relate to. (It is true that some versions add a hint of "reality" to the situation by the conjunction: "and discover the whole self, which includes the other," or again, insights of "mind-expanding visions of being one with all," which seem to fit so poorly with the bias toward "doing" that tends to dominate American and industrial societies.[4])

Certain science fiction short stories (books and films, too) provide insight into both the issues involved in the problem area and the strengths and the weaknesses of these models proposed as solutions. Several assumptions, difficulties, and consequences of the Operational-Behavioral/Functional-Mechanical model are exemplified in Isaac Asimov's "Evidence."[5]

The counter to this model is "a sense of purpose," for, contrary to what seems the dominant interpretation in our society, "fulfilling a function" does not guarantee a sense of purpose to a person. This is especially true when a person identifies with the function he or she performs and then finds that some mechanical entity can also fulfill that function. In such cases many persons have become confused, suffered a loss of their individual "reason for being," and experienced these shocks as dimensions of the disintegration of self and self-concept.

Jack Williamson's "With Folded Hands"[6] is unsurpassed in bringing these experiences and the place of "purpose" into focus. Ursula K. Le Guin's "Nine Lives"[7] presents a striking case of a multiple self, one which is seemingly self-sufficient and operating harmoniously, each part knowing fully all other parts. This is the kind of ideal situation or experience sought by so many by trying to discover the inner self and become totally aware of the dimensions of the self. That dimension beyond the self—the other—ignored by both the model and the multiple self in Le Guin's story, becomes highlighted through the turn of events as the sole reference through which the individual can achieve his orientation, his social and human existence.

OPERATIONAL-BEHAVIORAL/FUNCTIONAL-MECHANICAL MODEL

What is it to be a human being? A human being displays goal-oriented behavior; problem solving ability; ability to learn and change, to meet new situations and new challenges; emotional control, although possession of emotion-tempered reactions may be appropriate; acceptance of and fulfillment of responsibilities not only to self and family but to others in society, (that is, not selfishness but social obligation or altruism); and a concern for the rights and welfare of others. The exceptional human being follows not only social mores but the highest ideals of the most rigid moral systems that mankind has devised. This is a person who can and does "hold to his or her principles," not out of stubbornness but out of a commitment to what is right. Such a person knows himself or herself well enough to avoid being swayed by insecurities, petty squabbles, or the persecution of others, and would not feel threatened by opposition.

As impressive as this list may be, several troubling questions arise. How would one report from within oneself concerning the possession or the nonpossession of these qualities? But suppose we consider rather, how we would recognize them in another. What would we consider as evidence that the other was, indeed, a human being? Or, how would you prove conclusively that another was not a complicated, quite sophisticated machine or robot, its existence explicable in terms of electromechanical laws and publicly observable behavioral principles? Or, how could someone else prove this of you without your cooperation? This is a central concern in Asimov's story "Evidence."

The story is set in a society in which technological capability has far outdistanced social adjustment to that level of technology, and rigid controls have been placed on the appearance and use of robots. Robots must be used only for certain functions, in certain places on certain planets, and must not resemble or behave too similarly to human beings. In short, human beings enjoy the benefits of robots but at the same time fear robots.

A political campaign for the mayoralty is beginning. Candidate Quinn brings the charge to Mr. Lanning (Director-Emeritus of Research for U.S. Robots & Mechanical Men Corporation), that the candidate for mayor and present district attorney, Stephen Byerley, is a robot. Quinn challenges Lanning to prove that Byerley is not a robot, or U.S. Robots will be destroyed by the public outcry when Quinn announces his news. The problem is finding adequate evidence to determine conclusively whether Byerley is a robot or is not a robot (and thereby is a human being).

What about his records? Apparently he came on the scene as a public figure only three years ago, but records are found that give Byerley a full biography from birth to three years ago. Quinn pushes the matter of the district attorney's current behavior: he never eats, he never drinks, and he never sleeps. When Lanning and Robopsychologist Susan Calvin visit and confront Byerley with these charges, he quickly and in good humor points out the faulty logic involved, that because he has not been seen to do these things in public, it does not follow that he does not do them at all. Personal preference or private behavior are sufficient to explain this charge. Will he eat in public to prove the point, then? No. Byerley does take a bite from the apple which Calvin brought to his office, but both he and she recognize that this proves nothing—for any robot as sophisticated as Byerley is supposed to be would have provisions for these and all other normal biological functions, just in case.

Calvin later spells out to Quinn and Lanning that there are only two ways to decide the issue: the physical test (either "dissect him or use an X-ray") or the psychological (study his behavior). If Byerley follows the Laws of Robotics,[8] this will not prove that he is a robot; however, if he breaks the Laws of Robotics, it will prove he is not a robot.

Of course, this is not what Mr. Quinn wants proved for his campaign, but for our purposes, Robopsychologist Calvin's explanation of the matter is most interesting. Following the Laws of Robotics will not prove that Byerley is a robot because these rules "are the essential guiding principles of a good many of the world's ethical systems."[9] The Three Laws of Robotics are:

1 – A robot may not injure a human being, or, through inaction, allow a human being to come to harm.

2 – A robot must obey the orders given it by human beings except where such orders would conflict with the First Law.

3 – A robot must protect its own existence as long as such protection does not conflict with the First or Second Law.

Handbook of Robotics,
56th Edition, 2058 A.D.[10]

"To put it simply," says Dr. Calvin, "if Byerley follows all the Rules of Robotics, he may be a robot, or may simply be a very good man."[11]

Byerley's record as district attorney proves to be spotless. He has never asked for the death penalty; he has prosecuted those who would have done more harm to human beings if left unprosecuted; and he has headed various humane reforms including the attempt to replace capital punishment with rehabilitation and strong support of institutions studying ways to eliminate crime through neurophysiological means. Calvin informs Quinn, "Actions such as his could come only from a robot, or from a very honorable and decent human being. But you see, you just can't differentiate between a robot and the very best of humans."[12]

Frustrated, Quinn goes public with the wild charge, and Byerley is served with a court order to search his premises. When the warrant is served, Byerley permits the thorough search of his premises but does not agree to an examination of his "person." He has been elected and serves as district attorney – robots have no citizen or social rights in this society. The court order implicitly recognizes Byerley as a human being, a legal person, and as one who owns property. He has a psychiatric certificate proving that he is "a citizen of adult responsibility." What is being attempted, he points out, is a violation of his "Right of Privacy" as guaranteed by "the Regional Articles." In spite of his rights, the physical test is carried out, or rather attempted; the Quinn official snaps a form of x-ray scan of Byerley. That official, along with Quinn, later discovers, however, that Byerley was wearing a ray scan blocking body shield. So the attempt at the physical test fails to provide useful evidence.

The psychological test continues, but Byerley refuses to be baited, all the while letting Quinn bring Byerley's name into national, regional, and world headlines. The final stage of the psychological test is set at the last and almost uncontrollable political rally of the campaign. There, before television cameras, reporters, fanatics who violently oppose robots, and with Dr. Calvin in the background, Byerley—against his campaign manager's advice, who fears what the hostile crowd will do to his candidate—comes out to speak.

He calmly faces the hostility, and then has a confrontation with a particularly obnoxious heckler, whom he dramatically invites to the elevated porch. The heckler dares, his chin thrust out, "Hit me! You say you're not a robot. Prove it. You can't hit a human being, you monster." Tension mounts. The abusive, tempting challenge is hurled again. Byerley deliberately swings a clenched fist to that chin, collapsing the heckler—and the rally. Says Dr. Calvin to reporters as she walks away, "He's human."

Byerley wins the mayoralty. Then Robopsycholgist Calvin casually drops by to visit the new mayor and quietly tells him a story, which ends with a point that had been overlooked: "I mean there is one time when a robot may strike a human being without breaking the First Law. Just one time . . . when the human to be struck is merely another robot."[13]

Was the great Byerley, who went on to become regional co-ordinator and then the first world co-ordinator, simply a robot? Dr. Calvin replies to her interviewer, "Oh, there's no way of ever finding out. I think he was. But when he decided to die, he had himself atomized, so that there will never be any legal proof. Besides, what difference would it make?"[14]

What is it to be a human being? We began by believing that a human being is a person. Machines are not persons. A human being is different from a machine. But now it seems that based on the Behavioral/ Mechanical model, and the story, "Evidence," you can't tell them apart. Besides, what difference would it make?

For many people, it would make all the difference, although most would be hard pressed to come up with a feasible alternative on short notice. Difficulties include the problem of how we know the other (another human being), if not by observable behavior, operations performed, functions fulfilled, and mobility and actions which can be electromechanically explained. Is there nothing more, no human self which serves as one's core structure for self-identity? If it were not for the other, how could I find evidence of a difference, evidence of a self for or within me?

The most enthusiastic supporters of this model draw the conclusion clearly: there is no mysterious self; or, more accurately, no notion of such self is needed to adequately study and/or to alter those functioning processes.

But many people reject such a conclusion and point out that this model ignores that which a human being cannot do without—the self, that which can feel emotions and persist through a sense of purpose.

Here common sense and several critical studies may find agreement: machines serve functions but human beings have (choose, select, find meaning for life and death in) purposes. Within our culture, purpose has been blended in a rather confused way with happiness and immediate gratification of desires, to the point that they are often considered inseparable, as if they constituted a single, simple concept.

Jack Williamson's story, "With Folded Hands," provides an excellent setting to show that a sense of purpose is important to human beings, and that need-fulfillment, construed as happiness, is not necessarily the same as a sense of purpose.

Williamson's story is about the invasion of a society, which is one more step in a series of planetary invasions by a "race" of creatures. The kicker is that these creatures are humanoids (Williamson's term; others may refer to them as "robots") and the humanoids are really perfect— all knowing, all powerful, and committed to following a totally altruistic Prime Directive: "Our function is to serve and obey, and guard men from harm. It is no longer necessary for men to care for themselves, because we exist to insure their safety and happiness."[15]

At last, one might think, our dreams have been answered: there is leisure time to enjoy life with no need for pointless and endless work, all needs and wants are satisfied, and total safety is guaranteed. It's not quite that simple, however, as members of Mr. Underhill's society find out and Mr. Sledge, the creator of the humanoids, discovers early in the story.

Mr. Underhill sells "mechanicals," rather clumsy automatized creations, to assist in household work and other services. His life and livelihood are invaded by a competitor—or so it seems at first—who has an endless supply of streamlined, efficient, unbelievably highly skilled humanoids; they sell themselves, come on a free trial basis, and cost nothing. The range of services which they can provide is seemingly without limit.

Underhill has orders rejected and models of old mechanicals brought back, has no money to pay for a new order (which is delivered by humanoids, who have taken over delivery services), is refused extension of his loan (by humanoids, who have taken over banking services—a bit redundant anyway, except for stubborn Underhill, since free services do not require money), is stopped by a humanoid policeman (yes, police services, too), and finds that his wife has accepted a humanoid "free trial" service in their home. He stubbornly refuses to yield to their gentle reason, as they explain that he should do as others have done, that is, sign over a waiver of his business to them, since there is no longer need for private enterprise. Humanoids have taken over the court system also, as Underhill and Mr. Sledge find out.

Mr. Sledge is a boarder at the Underhills'; at first Underhill thinks he's just another crackpot like most of the others his wife has taken in. But he comes to realize that Sledge is far from what he initially thought; actually Sledge is a genius, and the creator of the humanoids. But now Sledge, ill and alone, is trying to develop a means to stop what he created.

Sledge survived a series of wars that killed most of the people on several planets, including the woman he loved. Deciding that humankind was incapable of governing itself, acting in its own best interest he creates a race of beings to protect humankind from itself. This was the reason for the creation of humanoids: to follow the totally altruistic Prime Directive; to serve and obey and guard humans from harm; and to insure human safety and happiness. Sledge carefully arranges intricate protection devices around the central intelligence center once the directive is set. The humanoids make more of their kind and their services spread.

Only gradually, and too late, does Sledge realize that his altruistic creations are out of control, and that their service does not result in human happiness. The latter dawns on him when he sees one human being (of several over the years, he learns) who has endured agonies beyond normal human capacities to find Sledge and kill him for what he has created and imposed upon humankind.

Through the experiences of Underhill, this process of awareness is repeated in his society. Leisure and need-fulfillment, so prized at first, become boring to his wife; his children forsake the practice of music in discouragement, for the perfect humanoids can play music perfectly. Underhill no longer has the struggle or the challenge of his business. In their lives and in their society, *all* potentially harmful objects and activities are withdrawn from humans and are replaced by the *services* of the all-good and all-powerful humanoids. But where is the anticipated happiness?

Underhill receives the full picture when Sledge, whom he had been assisting, fails to stop the humanoids by the complicated transmission system he had constructed. That overt act is the humanoids' signal to break in and dismantle the equipment; they have known all along but have respected Sledge's immunity (which he had programmed into the original intelligence bank). They still respect it for Sledge's person, for they do not interfere as the old man's heart gives in to the shock of defeat. Finally, he gasps consent to their services, and they quickly take him away.

When Underhill sees him later in the hospital, Sledge is seemingly well and happy; he laughs and praises the humanoids and cannot imagine how he could have ever opposed these wonderful beings. It must have been the result of that tumor which they removed from his brain.

Underhill looks at the scar on Sledge's head and knows that if all else fails, the humanoids insure man's "safety and happiness" by skilled brain surgery. Now Sledge is both safe and happy.

On the way home, Underhill's perceptive humanoid driver sees his terrified behavior and asks, "What is the matter, Mr. Underhill? Are you unwell?"

> "No, there's nothing wrong with me," he gasped desperately. "I've just found out that I'm perfectly happy, under the Prime Directive. Everything is absolutely wonderful." His voice came dry and hoarse and wild. "You won't have to operate on me . . ." His futile hands clenched and relaxed again, folded on his knees. There was nothing left to do.[16]

There is a set of double meanings in this story and the closing. Underhill (humankind) is perfectly happy without the help of the humanoids—without the brain surgery, which indicates the irony of the term happiness, and the services or "functions" carried on in society by the humanoids, which have successfully taken away humankind's sense of purpose.

The folded hands and the resigned remark "there was nothing left to do" speak to the same point: when a human being is totally safe through the curtailment of all his or her "normal" activities, when we are served in such a fashion and with an enforced leisure that humanity is dehumanized, our sense of purpose, of self, and of service to others are all mutilated or destroyed. The human identity and the sense of individual and social worth seem to be bound to these traits, and they, too, are destroyed.[17]

INNER-SELF DISCOVERY MODEL

What is it to be a human being, to be an individual, to be a self? One probes the areas of one's self, finding more levels and aspects of self, discovering the formerly unknown within, coming to recognize the multiple selves that one is. Through this one achieves *self-realization*, wherein an enriched relationship of all dimensions of the self interact and operate together harmoniously. One is no longer split within one-self but whole, united, for the multiple aspects interpenetrate and are in full awareness of one another. Here one realizes a full consciousness of self, seen and lived from within.

Ursula Le Guin's story, "Nine Lives," presents a basis both for exam-ining the goals and for noting the shortcomings of this model. Two in-dividuals, Martin and Pugh, have spent years on an inhospitable planet, mining the ore necessary for the normal activities of civilization on their home planet. At last additional personnel, other humans, are on their way to assist the two lonely miners. They face the situation with a mixture of joy at the prospect of seeing human faces again and of misgiving at the prospect of meeting people who will be strangers. Briefly, but emphatically, Le Guin sets the mood:

> It is hard to meet a stranger. Even the greatest extrovert meeting even the meekest stranger knows a certain dread, though he may not know he knows it. Will he make a fool of me wreck my image of myself in-vade me destroy me change me? Will he be different from me? Yes, that he will. There's the terrible thing: the strangeness of the stranger.
>
> After two years on a dead planet, and the last half year isolated as a team of two, oneself and one other, after that it's even harder to meet a stranger, however welcome he may be. You're out of the habit of differ-ence, you've lost the touch; and so the fear revives, the primitive anxi-ety, the old dread.[18]

How strange the stranger, how different, hits Pugh and Martin when the crew comes out of the ship: ten individuals who share the same eyes, the same smile, the same body—almost but not quite, for five are males and five are females— a ten-clone. Technological shock strikes: here are ten beings originating from the intestinal cell(s) of a sin-gle individual, their genetic substance "identical," and now their behav-ior, mannerisms, reactions, and appearance so close to being identical that Pugh and Martin see them as not only the same but ten of the same.

Originating from the cells of a genius, one John Chow ("We *are* John Chow"), these ten were trained in different specialities, but by nature think alike, cooperate, and work together "as one." Misunderstandings seldom occur and explanations are unnecessary for this strange but remarkably efficient "team," this unit of multiple selves. "They" accomplish tasks easily and quickly which would take "separate individuals" much more time and difficulty (loss of effort) to do. "They" suffer no troubled emotions about such things as being "self-conscious" about their actions or behavior; the "singletons" Pugh and Martin note this in observing, among other things, the sexual behavior of pairs of the clone.

Pugh and Martin, though treated courteously, are ever on the outside, not a part of but distinctly apart from, the being, behavior, and awareness of the John Chow clone of ten who are different only in training and their middle names. Pugh and Martin wonder what it must be like, for example, to "love your-self," or to find nine "Yea's" for your every idea, seconds for your every motion, whether "repetition of the individual negate(s) individuality," and what it must be like for your skin to be literally my skin, and for the neighbor to be the self, and "never to be in pain alone."

Well they might wonder such things, for normal individuals, "singletons" like Martin and Pugh, have not known, and could never know, what these experiences are like; Martin and Pugh are outsiders, "others" — the other, not really needed in any significant sense by such a self-sufficient "multiple self" as the ten-clone John Chow.

An earthquake occurs. The ten-clone is missing. Martin and Pugh race to the collapsed mine, but manage to find only two bodies; only one is still alive. The single survivor is Kaph, but he is in deep shock. Kaph, "alone" for the first time, has no will to live; he dies the death of his nine fellow clones or selves, so Pugh and Martin deduce. By extraordinary effort Pugh and Martin revive Kaph from each of these deaths. Nine lives gone, nine deaths experienced within himself — relived, so to speak — Kaph laments that he is nine-tenths dead: "There is not enough of me left alive."

Kaph does return to functioning but in a nonhuman, machinelike fashion. Martin and Pugh are there, to be sure, but hardly for Kaph, for "he never had to see anyone else before" since he had "never known anyone but himself." Kaph begins to learn, or rather, relearn things which he strangely seems to have forgotten. Pugh risks his life in a fran-

tic search for and successful attempt to save Martin. Later Kaph seems
to change; after Martin is asleep, Kaph asks Pugh, "Do you love Martin?" Yes. "How can you . . .? How do you . . .?"

A relief crew is coming—a twelve-clone, "a multiple self of which
Kaph was not part." In his loneliness and dawning awareness, Kaph
looked at Pugh "and saw the thing he had never seen before: saw him:
saw Owen Pugh, the other, the stranger who held his hand out in the
dark."[1]

Kaph saw at last what many proponents of the Inner-Self Discovery
model fail to see, namely that, regardless of the thrill of self-discovery
and the imagined self-sufficiency of the harmoniously operating aspects
of the multiple self, this is inadequate. There is the other. As long as we
exist as social beings, the other must be taken into account; this is the
point of my indicating earlier that "the problem of the self" and "the
problem of others" are correlated, two poles of an interrelated problem.

Similarly, forms of the Operational-Behavioral/Functional-
Mechanical model which overlook or ignore the necessity of the "self"
and a sense of purpose for that self are inadequate. A more satisfactory
solution to this problem, it seems to me, would include a balanced response to and treatment of these two dimensions, self and other. And
this solution should have as significant components a sense of purpose
and a sense of individual and social worth.

12.

The Absurdity of Sartre's Ontology: A Response by Ursula K. Le Guin

WAYNE COGELL

Wayne Cogell received his doctorate from the University of Missouri-Columbia and is now associate professor of philosophy at the University of Missouri-Rolla, where he has been since 1967.

Cogell's primary philosophical interests are in the areas of aesthetics (especially philosophy in literature), philosophical psychology and existentialism, and ethics. But his work in philosophy and science fiction has contributed as much—or more—to this young field as anyone's. This is apparent in his numerous presentations to professional organizations and published essays in the field, and especially in his continuing role in the Science Fiction Research Association, without which this book might never have been completed. Cogell invited me to present a paper at the 1978 meetings of that organization, where I met Monte Cook and Bob Pielke as well as Cogell himself. It was also there that I was invited to put together a program for the 1979 Popular Culture Association Convention. Most of the remaining essays were included as contributions to the convention.

Moreover, I met a number of my favorite authors at

those meetings, including Gordon Dickson, Joe
Haldeman, Jack Williamson, Gene Wolfe, Brian Aldiss,
and Ursula K. Le Guin, whose clever story "A Trip to the
Head" Cogell uses in the following essay to critique
Jean-Paul Sartre's existential ontology.

"A Trip to the Head" is a short story by Ursula K. Le Guin that presents a *reductio ad absurdum* of the existential philosophy of Jean Paul Sartre and much more.[1] I will only discuss the *reductio* in this paper.

Le Guin calls attention to three absurdities in Sartre's philosophy: first, the arbitrariness and lack of firm grounds in Sartre's account of human choice, which makes ethics meaningless; second, the exclusive emphasis on subjective time, which results in solipsism; and third, the emphasis on self-created essence, which makes significant interpersonal human relations impossible.

Sartre's philosophy as presented in *Being and Nothingness* has the following features: (1) a being-in-itself, which is given complete in essence and act; (2) a phenomenological approach, which results in the claim that all is given in the phenomenal appearances of things; (3) a being-for-itself, which is consciousness in process of projecting meanings on things and itself; and (4) a being-for-others, which is viewed as a direct threat to personal freedom. I will detail the features of Sartre's ontology and Le Guin's response to them.[2]

Sartre conceives of being-in-itself (*en soi*) as an absolute plenum with no potency and no real relations to anything else.[3] It is complete because its essence is given in its actual, particular existence, as exemplified by a table or a rock. The result is a finished continuum fully actualized and totally complete, lacking all power and potency. Such a view is similar to Heidegger's suggestion that there is a subhuman existence, a determinate being-on-hand (*Vorhandensein*) which is something finished and simply there. According to Sartre, beings-in-themselves, such as trees and fawns, are completely given with an essence that indicates what they are. They are complete in act and therefore cannot change or cause anything.

Sartre is, like other existentialists before him, primarily interested in the concrete data of experience as they actually appear.[4] He claims to follow a purely descriptive, phenomenological approach. Anxious to reject the Kantian conception of a noumenal thing-in-itself behind the phenomena, Sartre asserts that things appear only in perception and that perceptions associated with them exhaust all positive reality. The appearances of things are their reality. This identifies being with the succession of its finished appearances.

According to Sartre, a real thing whose existence is presented phenomenologically can never be exhausted by any concept invented by men. There will always be properties in excess of anything the concept may imply.

In *Nausea*, the diary entry for Wednesday 6:00 P.M. indicates "the world of explanations and reasons is not the world of existence."[5] The chestnut tree is not a "chestnut tree" since the latter fails, like any general label, to capture the superabundant overflowing of the reality to which it is lamely applied. The basic theme which Sartre develops is that the structures of consciousness are different than the structures of the objects of consciousness.

In contrast to being-in-itself and the phenomenal appearances of things, a human being is a being-for-itself *(pour soi)*.[6] Being-for-itself is a potential nothingness. As potential nothingness, it is characterized as having its existence precede its essence and as having the capacity of consciousness, which is the power of negation.

Unlike being-in-itself, human beings find that they exist but do not understand why. They are not born with meaning or purpose – this they must define for themselves; they must create their essence. They must also create their world; since the realm of being is a dense field without distinction, there is no determinate structure or finite difference. Except as those distinctions are made by the projects of the being-for-itself, the world is not intelligible. This potential to create the world applies also to the self and resides in the capacity of consciousness.

The capacity of consciousness is the power of negations, that is, the ability to conceive of things as they are not. If being-in-itself is fully in act, it cannot be deprived of anything it requires; it is complete within itself. Therefore, negation and privation have no ground in being, but must be referred to the negativity of human consciousness.

Perceptions, for example, are given to consciousness as complete and only as what they are: a tree is given as branch, leaf, etc. The ability to conceive of a given tree in early spring as not given, cut down, or as bearing fruit, is the human power of negation as a projection on the given. Human consciousness as the power of negation operates as a projection on being-in-itself and being-for-itself. When consciousness results in a projection, a new reality is created.

Another aspect of Sartre's ontology is "being-for-others" (*autrui*).[7] The temporalized world of being-for-itself is an insulated world. Into the world of being-for-itself, the others make their appearance. The interrelation of personal selves is disclosed in shame. Through shame I discover simultaneously the other and an aspect of my being. I am ashamed of my self before the other. The other reveals myself to me.

I need the other, Sartre maintains, in order to realize fully all the structures of my being. Other people make me aware of myself; they make me see how what I am doing is to be described. They label me as stupid, clever, dishonest. Other people's descriptions of my acts modify my view of myself. For example, the realization that other people regard me as predictably unpunctual modifies my view of myself, since from my own point of view each instance of unpunctuality is just a matter of chance, just bad luck.

Another way in which the other is disclosed is through "the look."[8] According to Sartre, "the look" of the other erupts into my world, decentralizes and dissolves it and, by reference to his own projects, reconstitutes it and the freedom which I experience. The other is apprehended as one who is about to steal my world, suck me into the orbit of his concerns and reduce me to the mode of being-in-itself, to an object or thing.

Through *my* look I can seek to shatter the world of the other and divest him of his subjective freedom, the freedom to decide for himself his future. I seek to remove the other from my world and put him out of play, but this can never succeed. I encounter the other; I do not constitute him. The other remains, threatening to counterattack. Thus there results a constant cycle of mutual objectivization.

The upshot of all this is an irreconcilable conflict between the self and the other with a consequent breakdown of all communication. Alienation has the last word in Sartre's doctrine of inter-subjectivity. The search for a positive doctrine of community is not part of Sartre's philosophy. All forms of "being-with" find their common denominator in an alienating "being-for."

Sartre's account of the constitutive structure of human existence has the significant implication that man has no common nature or essence. He makes himself into what he is by the projects which he chooses. Man is condemned to freedom, although he desires to be a being-in-itself, complete in essence.

Human action, however, is not a mode of being, but rather a mode of negativity. It is always pursuing itself, but never achieving unity. Any choice, for example, is a flight into the future from the present. No sooner is it realized than it must be rejected to preserve the fluid negativity of being-for-itself. Human beings can never rest; personal nothingness, incompleteness, and freedom are their existential predicament.

How does Le Guin represent and respond to Sartre's existential theory of man?

In "A Trip to the Head"⁹ Le Guin presents to the reader endless Sartrian absurdities to study. She has two characters who do not know their own names or identities; an island, England, which has sunk; arbitrary jumps in time of twenty to thirty years in order that Ralph's sexual appetite may be satisfied; a trip in a sewer pipe; the disappearance of The Other for no apparent reason; and Ralph's assertion that he is Lewis D. Charles (but alas, he has given the wrong name, just as Sartre has given a wrong description of things).

These actions are meaningless, silly, inconsequential, and absurd. Throughout her story Le Guin has, in contrast to Sartre's view, the natural, uniform movement of the world turning on its axis. Nature is there in the forest with "mild eyes" unaffected by these Sartrian absurd contingencies.

Le Guin's two characters (Blank and The Other) are set in an absurd world entangled with the three aspects of Sartre's ontology: a given world of a being-in-itself, a being-for-itself, and a being-for-others. The world is absurd.

In Zambia men are rolling down hills inside barrels as training for space flight. Israel and Egypt have defoliated each other's deserts. The *Reader's*

Digest has bought a controlling interest in the United States of America/General Mills combine. The population of the earth is increasing by thirty billion every Thursday. Mrs. Jacqueline Kennedy Onassis will marry Mao Tse-tung on Saturday in search of security, and Russia has contaminated Mars with breadmold.[10]

Le Guin concretely shows what Sartre's world would be like. She not only satirically displays Sartre's philosophy but asserts, through her use of literary devices, that his view is empirically inadequate.

Le Guin presents Blank as a character unaware of where he is or who he is. He recognizes that he has a body (being-in-itself) but he is "a blank, a cipher, an X." She says, "He had a body and all that, but he had no who." Because he has no common nature or essence, Blank must make himself. The Other suggests that he could take any name or label, like Disposable, but Blank wants to know his real name. He faces the question squarely. "How can I say who I am when I can't say what I am?"

The Other suggests, "It's what you do that counts," and Blank immediately stands up and declares that he will exist and call himself "Ralph."

What follows is Blank's attempt at a Sartrian definition of himself. He is a Yankee landowner hopelessly, romantically in love with a Southern lady, Amanda, who does not understand what he desires when he says, "I never wanted anything but you, my white lily, my little rebel! I want you! I want you! Amanda! Say you will be my wife!" Suddenly there is a leap of twenty or thirty years and Ralph's desires are made clear to Amanda. Now Amanda is knees up, naked against a pecan tree; she and Blank couple and climax is achieved.

In response to Sartre's position Le Guin has shown one absurdity in his existential theory of man: the supposed arbitrariness and the lack of firm grounds for human choice. In trying to create myself by the projects which I chose, according to Sartre, whether I die for justice or drink at a bar is a matter of indifference.

The arbitrariness of Blank's choice to be Ralph is followed by an arbitrariness of location, time, and character. Blank's frustration is remedied with a sudden leap of twenty or thirty years. The lack of firm grounds for his choice is clearly illustrated by Le Guin. When Blank returns to the original setting with The Other, he is confused about his sex. "Am I a man?" inquires Blank. "And are you a woman?"

Another absurdity in Sartre's existential theory of man, resulting from the lack of firm grounds for human choice, is that no account of human ethics is possible. Since man has no stable nature, since he possesses no constant tendencies, and since he is condemned to no rest, personal nothingness, and freedom, it does not make sense to provide changeless norms to which he must conform his conduct. In fact if Sartre is right, all regrets must be momentarily felt but not understood since they are not the result of anything in the person. Thus Le Guin has Blank feel sorry for sexually abusing The Other but immediately moves on to a new project.

Another absurdity results in Sartre's account of being-for-itself as consciousness because of his emphasis on subjective time. According to this doctrine, human consciousness temporalizes itself through an integral order of qualitative changes in which the past that I have been and the future project that I will be are integrated in the present consciousness of my becoming.

Le Guin shows the effect of Sartre's emphasis on subjective time when Blank declares, "I'm on some kind of trip." He is paddling his canoe against the current, uphill, enclosed in a concrete sewer pipe. It's hard work but his canoe keeps gliding forward upriver as the black shining water moves back down. He can't say anything; he has no idea of where he is or if he is moving forward or only hanging still.

It is a consequence of Sartre's emphasis on consciousness that man is caught in solipsism. What one knows is limited to the sewer pipe of his consciousness in which he glides, not knowing if he is moving forward or hanging still.

Le Guin does not totally disagree with this analysis of subjective time. What she regards as wrong is Sartre's disregard for the importance of world-time. For Le Guin, there is also a flux of world-time which is sweeping the stars, the planets, and a person's life in a single irreversible direction. In terms of Sartre's position, however, man is enclosed in his own stream of consciousness without any possible passage to the external world.

In "A Trip to the Head," Le Guin confronts the problem of the Other from the beginning of the story: "As Jean Paul Sartre has said in his lovable way, Hell is other people." The Other is a threat to Blank's being but is needed to aid in his creation of his essence. The Other is willing to place any label on Blank.

From Blank's view The Other is used to prove his being in sexual intercourse, which he views as "having and acting in its intensest form." The Other tries to show that it matters which man and which woman are involved together with their particular, unique, characteristics. "For instance," The Other says, "what if Amanda was black?"

Finally, when Blank realizes that he is nothing, the Other suggests that he might as well be Jean Paul Sartre. This suggestion drives Blank to a denial that results in his asserting that he is Lewis D. Charles, at which point The Other disappears. "Lewis D. Charles looked in the red eye of the west and the dark eye of the east. He shouted aloud, 'Come back! Please come back!' "

If Sartre's account of man is correct then, as Le Guin properly points out, to create oneself is to destroy the other, and each person is alone. Love, friendship, and devoted cooperation for common ends are excluded *a priori*. All of this Le Guin views as dubious.

The consequence of Sartre's philosophy is that all that is given in the phenomenal appearances of things is contingent. In the classical discussion of being, thinkability, necessity, contingency, meaning, truth, and that which is accidental intersect in the doctrine of essence. Also the traditional account states that the existence of things does not form part of their essence. The definition of man—"Man is a rational animal"—indicates what man essentially is, independent of whether such a creature exists. The doctrine maintains as unthinkable that something should be human without being rational. (There is one exception in the tradition: the concept of God who exists necessarily, his existence being his essence). Thus the essence of a thing is logically prior to its existence.

In Sartre's philosophy of man, however, one's existence precedes his essence. Existence is always something literally extra. Hence the existence of a person is always logically superfluous and never part of the concept we may apply to him. What is absurd in Sartre's philosophy is that everything human is superfluous, because it is meaningless and contingent. However that which is merely contingent and without necessity is for Le Guin absurd, not merely silly or meaningless.

In "A Trip to the Head" Le Guin has Blank discover "I am myself," which rings as self-validating as the Cartesian *cogito ergo sum*.

"He knew it as well as he knew his own name," Le Guin says ironically. He is tied to world-time: "There he was," she writes, "The forest was there, root and branch." The paradox, however, is that he got the wrong name because "He had gone at it all wrong, backwards."

For Le Guin the world is not absurd; there are natural grounds for human choice which are found in the full history of an individual integrated in the present world flux. But there may be things hidden from view, such as internal structures of nature with "mild eyes" that look back at human beings from the "darkness of the trees." Le Guin's position here seems to be that each existing thing has finite structures which limit and act as its ontological ground; it has potencies which are marked by an absence of realization. Things can pass, turn away, or cease to be, but without the recognition of each living thing's finite structures, the fact of physical change and any view of nature becomes unintelligible and absurd.

> Under the trees Blank forgot his name again at once. He also forgot what he was looking for. What was it he had lost? He went deeper and deeper into shadows, under leaves, eastward, in the forest where nameless tigers burned.[11]

Le Guin would have us return to nature (as do the fawn and Blank), to nature the way things really are, nameless but not absurd.

13.

Grokking the Stranger

BY ROBERT G. PIELKE

*Robert Pielke received his bachelors degree in history
with a minor in philosophy at the University of
Maryland. He attended the Lutheran Theological
Seminary in Gettysburg, Pennsylvania, where he
received a bachelors of divinity (now called a masters of
divinity), and went on to complete his doctorate in
social ethics at the Department of Religion, Claremont
Graduate School.*

*Pielke has written a number of articles in a variety of
fields, but he is best known for his work in the fields of
ethics and social and political philosophy. He has
published a number of essays in the area of philosophy
and science fiction.*

*This paper concerns the appeal of the political views
found in the work of Robert Heinlein. An earlier version
was presented at the Popular Culture Association
Convention in Pittsburgh in 1978.*

*Pielke is now an assistant professor of philosophy
and religion (teaching courses in both areas) at George
Mason University in Fairfax, Virginia, where he has
been since 1970.*

No one has ever accused Robert A. Heinlein of writing great literature, but he has certainly been guilty of achieving extreme popularity.
Ever since 1929, when his first short stories were published, his prolific
work has been assured of a wide and enthusiastic audience.

His most controversial and perhaps best work is the 1962 Winner of
the Hugo Award, *Stranger in a Strange Land.* As an indication of its
popularity, its readers have extended far beyond the typical science fiction following, attracting an almost cultlike devotion from many of
them. The most notorious example of this was its use (or rather misuse) by the Manson family.

Of more significance and interest, however, has been its continuing
appeal for two apparently conflicting and rather amorphous groups:
the extreme right and its counterpart on the extreme left. I intend to
explore what it is about the book that both groups find appealing and
to explain how this is possible.

Clearly, its appeal is ideological. Both groups find their political and
social beliefs mirrored and idealized to such an extent that *Stranger in a
Strange Land* has become an almost canonical portrayal of their goals.
This, of course, is not in any way an explanation; it's merely a restate-
ment of the problem. We need to know how this kind of ideological
harmony can exist between the two groups, when they are at the same
time involved in sharp ideological conflicts. What sense can this possibly make?

From my perspective, the best way to comprehend this seemingly
paradoxical relationship is through a philosophical analysis of Heinlein's ideas. No other discipline or methodology is so aptly suited to
deal specifically with ideas, and the most relevant philosophical questions in this case are those raised into the related areas of ethics and political philosophy.

In the first section, I'll make use of several philosophical distinctions
in order to describe the differences between these two political extremes and show how they are manifest in *Stranger in a Strange Land.*
The second section will continue the philosophical characterization by
explaining how and why there can be harmony between them. In the
concluding section, I'll venture a few interpretive remarks about the
meaning of the biblically derived title, "Stranger in a Strange Land,"

showing how it relates to the philosophical analysis of the first two sections.

The Apparent Conflict

The political labels "right" and "left" have become virtually useless as analytic tools, as have the terms "conservative" and "liberal." In order to restore the typological value they ought to have, I propose to identify the latter pair as deontological (conservative) and teleological (liberal) ethical reasoning respectively. With the same purpose in mind, the first pair will then be understood to indicate the affirmation (right) and rejection (left) of psychological egoism.

I regard these proposals as more than merely stipulative definitions, but a defense of their reportive character will have to be undertaken elsewhere. In any case, these proposed meanings have the virtue of being descriptive and not covertly evaluative as their frequent use would have us believe.

As descriptive labels, these terms enable us to see a much more complex relationship between the extreme left and right than a simple dichotomy might indicate. For one thing, we are accustomed to thinking of conservativism and the right as synonymous; so too with liberalism and the left. My proposals split these pairs, making possible a total of four combinations: liberal left, liberal right, conservative left, and conservative right. These, I think, quite accurately represent the varied political phenomena we actually experience. For example, some utilitarians accept and others reject the notion that man is an innately self-interested, isolated creature (Hobbes and Mill). Likewise, the proponents of natural or intrinsic rightness differ on the question of society's being artificial, as psychological egoists would have it, or natural, as their opponents believe (Locke and Rousseau).

As I hope to demonstrate, this four-fold differentiation will finally enable us to understand the anomaly of the widespread appeal of *Stranger in a Strange Land.* I think it can also help us to understand American political life as a whole, but that is another matter.

Our perplexity is initially increased when the two groups to whom this book is so appealing are no longer identified simply as the extreme left and right, but as the extreme conservative left and the extreme liberal right. Their ideological split could hardly be more total. Not only do they conflict over whether humans are by nature isolated and self-seeking or social and concerned for others, but they're also antagonistic in terms of ethical reasoning. (I don't mean to imply, of course, that only these two groups and no others find the book appealing. But the fact that two so totally diverse ideological groups both find it to be an expression of their sociopolitical goals is certainly an item worth understanding.)

Each group finds its position represented in *Stranger in a Strange Land* through one of the two major characters. Jubal Harshaw, a character who appears in many of Heinlein's novels in one form or another as the author himself, represents the extreme liberal right. His liberal reasoning takes the form of ethical egoism, the moral injunction that every person should maximize his or her own good (not the total good, as in utilitarianism).

The very first reference to Jubal points out that he is a "rugged individualist," willing to do anything if it suited him.[1] His secluded hideaway in the Poconos is named Freedom Hall, where "everyone does as he pleases . . . then if he does something I don't like, I kick him the hell out."[2] The self is the sole legitimate moral authority; its will is supreme. "Nobody imposes on me against my will," he says.[3] Consequently "rights" cannot exist, other than as the right to pursue one's own interests, and Jubal's thinking is certainly in line with this.[4]

The major difficulty with this ethic, of course, is that self-defeating conflicts are inevitable: it can't be in the ethical egoist's interest for all others to seek their interests too. Realizing this, Jubal chooses to live alone as the logical extension of his self-proclaimed pessimism.[5] The inevitability of conflict makes isolation from others the only logical alternative to the unpleasant prospect of chaos.

The aspect of Jubal's character that I'm calling the right, the affirmation of psychological egoism, is just as clearly evident. "I'm suspicious of a disinterested interest," he says in reaction to an alleged concern for human rights. "You had better examine your motives, then judge which way you are going."[6] Continuing his appraisal of human motivations, he recalls, "I used to think I was serving humanity . Wand I pleasured in the thought. Then I discovered that humanity does not want to be served; on the contrary it resents any attempt to serve it. So now I do what pleases Jubal Harshaw."[7] This honesty about his own motivations has revealed to him what he regards as the true nature of everyone, yet few others realize it. Hence in proposing a toast, he solemnly intones, "Here's to our noble selves! There are damned few of us left."[8]

The other major character exemplifies the extreme conservative left. He is Valentine Michael Smith, a human being born on Mars and raised by the Martian "Old Ones."[9] His conservativism, or deontological reasoning, is such an overwhelming presence that it's likely to be overlooked. It has to do with his ability to "grok," perhaps the most significant concept in the book. More than merely intuitive insight, but certainly including it, grokking is the ability to empathize, to merge with, to become one with a person, object, or situation. The identification is so total that the true essence of the grokked object is known with absolute certainty.

Having had this capacity developed in him by the Martians, Mike is eventually able to know right, wrong, good, and bad with unerring accuracy, for these moral terms designate essential (but nonempirical) properties. As such their presence or absence must be intuited in some sense. When Jill (his nurse and friend) is threatened with a gun, "he grokked that this was one of the critical cusps in the growth of a being wherein contemplation must bring forth right action in order to permit further growth."[10] Later, he reveals that he knew (grokked) the gun to be a "bad thing."[11]

"Grokking wrongness" almost always leads to the "discorporation" of whatever it is that's bad or wrong; it is the rather drastic solution of being "sent elsewhere," as when Jubal's sanctuary is threatened.[12] Normative ethical judgments are based solely on intrinsic features, not on the amount of individual satisfaction likely to be achieved, as they are for Jubal.

Mike's view of human nature as being fundamentally social and co-operative, is, again, so obvious that it's easily missed. Self-seeking is simply not a possibility for him, and he assumes this to be true for all others as well. When Jubal tries to explain selfish lying to Mike, it is no easy task. "Mike's difficulty was that he didn't know what a lie was — definitions of 'lie' and 'falsehood' had been filed in his mind with no trace of grokking. One could 'speak wrongly' only by accident."[13] Of course for all those who have actualized their potentially harmonious nature (water brothers), such accidents simply didn't happen: "A water brother could not lead him into wrongful action."[14] There are no individual interests apart from and contrary to the social interest for Mike.

Thus in terms of both human nature and ethical reasoning, the two major characters are the very antithesis of each other. Therefore the book's odd appeal might be understood as simply the result of each antagonistic group having its own favorite character.

This, however, is not the case at all. Both characters are almost equally appealing to both groups! The next section will attempt to clarify what sense this can possibly make.

THE UNDERLYING HARMONY

The clue to the popularity of both characters with both groups lies in the fact that both groups are self-consciously extremists. I don't mean by this that they feel violence to be a morally desirable or permissible political tool. Rather, their extremism has to do with their optimistic views about the possibility of harmonious social relationships without any reliance on external controls; it's a *conceptual,* not a *tactical* extremism. As it turns out, this conceptual extreme makes violence not only unnecessary but morally repugnant as well.

Those of the extreme or optimistic right, unlike Jubal Harshaw as we first meet him, are highly confident that the universal pursuit of individual interests will not produce destructive conflicts. Rather, such interests are felt to be ultimately harmonious.

Various reasons have been cited to support this belief. The most famous, I suppose, is Adam Smith's "invisible hand," which apparently superimposes the necessary harmony. Others have had confidence in divine intervention or the free market system. Some even deny that real conflicts exist.

While Jubal is initially a pessimist in this regard, he slowly becomes convinced that a harmony of interests is possible after seeing what Mike has accomplished with his water brotherhood. By the end of the story his pessimism has been completely transformed into its opposite. Although Mike's accomplishments are clearly the catalyst for Jubal's transformation, we never really learn the source of his new optimism. It is crucial that the reader is allowed to supply his or her own interpretation as to its origin. In this way neither the left nor the right has to yield its view of human nature in order to respond favorably to Jubal's change, since an extremist attitude is consistent with both.

The source of Mike's initial optimism, on the other hand, is quite unambiguous—it's his belief in the innate goodness of humankind. Not only are humans a potentially cooperative species, but this potentiality can actually be brought to fruition. Thus Mike founds his Church of All Worlds, Inc. as the instrument of actualization. The phrase "Thou art God" epitomizes the goodness and oneness of all things, and the ability to grok reveals the truth of this insight and actualizes it as well.

So using the outward trappings of religion, Mike teaches man to grok. As with Jubal, however, there is a transformation. This time it's from a tremendously naive optimism to one which acknowledges the difficulty of the task. In his last conversation with Jubal before his martyrdom, he says, "Goodness is not enough, goodness is never enough. That was one of my first mistakes, because among Martians goodness and wisdom are identical. But not with us. . . . A hard, cold wisdom is required for goodness to accomplish good."[15]

And this wisdom he has derived from Jubal. Whereas he was once too optimistic, unaware of the "insanity" of man's jealousy and possessiveness, Jubal has unknowingly taught him to put his optimism in perspective. But the source of Mike's optimism has not clearly undergone a change, only its degree has changed; although someone on the right could make a plausible case that it had really been more than a change in degree. Again the uncertainty is the crucial thing, for it allows interpretations consistent with either perspective.

We have at the conclusion of the novel, then, two extremely (but not absurdly) optimistic characters who firmly believe for one reason or another that, eventually, people will be able to live together in harmony without the need for social controls. In other words, we are presented with a fictionalized account of anarchism, one which emphasizes the paramount importance of this high degree of confidence. Regardless of its source, an optimistic belief of this type is the necessary precondition for urging the goal of a stateless society.

In many ways, I feel that leaving the question of its source ambiguous is Heinlein's best touch. The views of both the right and the left are expressed in a way that clearly reveals their radical antagonism. Yet because of the ambiguity, we are left with the definite impression that even these differences are unimportant; for it's the *degree* of optimism that counts and not its *source*. This is all too often overlooked in defenses of anarchism, and overlooking it has had the unfortunate consequence of mistakenly equating anarchy with chaos.

By down-playing political-ethical reasoning and theories of human nature, Heinlein has highlighted the linchpin of all anarchistic thought. In so doing, *Stranger in a Strange Land* has become an ideological tract for the strangest of bedfellows. Though devotees of the book may disagree on virtually everything else, their enormous optimism about the possibililities of social life in the absence of a state renders these disagreements insignificant.

THE STRANGE LAND

At first glance, the title, *Stranger in a Strange Land,* seems to require no clarification whatsoever. After all, what else could it mean than a reference to Mike, a stranger in his own land which he naturally finds strange?

This deceptively simple answer fails to satisfy us, however, when we ask what it is that's so strange. Presumably, Mike is strange to humans because he was raised by Martians and thus is unfamiliar with his home planet and its biological, psychological, and social complexities. In effect he's an alien, and hence a stranger in the sense that anything alien is strange.

Yet if this is the case, then "in a strange land" becomes a meaningless redundancy. It's necessarily true that "aliens" are in "strange lands," otherwise they wouldn't be aliens. Now this may be all Heinlein intends with the phrase, but it's certainly not all that appears to me as a reader.

To me, the "land" (the earth and its human populace) is "strange" in and of itself – quite apart from its being made so by the juxtaposition of an alien's presence. The alien may point out what it is that's strange, but the strangeness is there for anyone who's sensitive enough to perceive it. In other words, the strangeness of the land is not simply and exclusively a function of Mike's being a stranger.

What makes the land strange in its own right (at least for me) is the contradiction between man's potential for harmony, peace, and mutual concern on the one hand and the actuality of his hatred, cruelty, and selfishness on the other. Heinlein is not the first to explore this, of course, nor will he be the last. But the lack of originality doesn't diminish its value.

In any case, just as Heinlein is suitably ambiguous concerning the source of man's potential good, he is almost totally silent on the source of his actual evil. Anarchists have traditionally cited the state and its laws, institutions, and/or customs as the major if not the exclusive causes for evil. And Heinlein would probably agree, but it doesn't seem to be of great importance to him. Pointing out the above disparity is apparently of far greater consequence. He wants to demonstrate how utterly strange, incomprehensible, and senseless it is that essential goodness should yield evil!

This idea is presupposed in the conversations between Jubal and Mike concerning what it means to be a human. Jubal finally boils it down to the notion that "man is the animal who laughs," an ability Mike had not learned from the Martians.[16] When mankind finally achieves humanity in this sense, it's precisely because the contradiction is perceived.

> I've found out why people laugh. They laugh because it hurts . . . because it's the only thing that'll make it stop hurting. . . . I saw all the mean and cruel and utterly unexplainable things I've seen and heard and read about in the time I've been with my own people – and suddenly it hurt so much I found myself laughing. . . . I had thought – I had been told – that a "funny" thing is a thing of goodness. It isn't. Not ever is it

funny to the person it happens to. . . . The goodness is in the laughing. I grok it is a bravery . . . and a sharing . . . against the pain and sorrow and defeat.[17]

Laughter, then, is the distinctly human response to the perception of the possibility of good and the actuality of evil. As Mike says,

On Mars there is *never* anything to laugh at. All the things that are funny to us humans [human evil] either cannot happen on Mars or are not permitted to happen . . . what you call "freedom" doesn't exist on Mars; everything is planned by the Old Ones—or the things that do happen on Mars which we laugh at here on Earth [natural evil] aren't funny because there is no wrongness about them.[18]

On Mars the contradiction does not exist; hence there is no possibility for laughter. The essential goodness of total sharing is an actuality for Martians. Intentional evil is completely unknown.

At this point Heinlein comes perilously close to a contradiction of his own. The lack of a contradiction on Mars is apparently purchased at the cost of freedom. If this is so, how can he at the same time urge more freedom, in the form of anarchy, as the solution for the contradiction among humans? Freedom is seemingly stressed as both the cause of and the solution for the problem of evil!

Heinlein's reasoning might be that more freedom for humans would have the same beneficial results as no freedom has had for Martians. After all, they are an essentially different species. Heinlein, however, doesn't pursue the thought any further, a fact which again allows for multiple interpretations. In any case, the question of freedom along with the contradiction between potentiality and actuality makes the land strange indeed.

Observations of this kind are not uncommon. Damon Knight, for example, sees Heinlein as both a radical empiricist and a mystic, a person whose worlds are forever optimistic and whose villains are unconvincing.[19] David Samuelson calls the work "Heinlein's most moving book, partly because of the tension between realities and wish-fulfillment."[20]

Most interesting to me, however, are the nonanalytic references to

both the book and the biblical phrase, and I'm sure there are many
more than those I've encountered. The phrase "I have been a stranger
in a strange land," emerges as a quotation from The Orange Catholic
Bible in Frank Herbert's *Dune*.[21] It's cited by a character who apparently sees the senselessness of using evil to accomplish good. Kilgore
Trout, a character in Kurt Vonnegut, Jr.'s *Breakfast of Champions*, is referred to as "a stranger in a strange land."[22] Here, the parallel with
Heinlein's usage virtually creates an identity: Trout is an innocent who
finds himself in an absurdly paradoxical world. Tom Wolfe, in *The
Electric Kool-Aid Acid Test*, observes that Ken Kesey's Merry Pranksters
saw themselves as Heinlein's stranger.[23] They even created a facsimile
of the Water Brotherhood's Nest as a haven in what was to them a
very joyful yet hostile land. Further, "grokking" was their adopted term
for total understanding, an ability which all people shared but which
they had not yet actualized.

In all of these cases, the phrase, "stranger in a strange land," allusions
to it, and analyses of it are intended to indicate a radical disjunction between actual and potential human relationships. Yet despite this contradiction, a mood of optimism prevails in both the biblical original as
well as in all of its derivative uses: for one reason or another, it's believed that the potential harmony can be actualized to some degree.

This brings us back to our earlier analysis. Those who feel that a high
degree of actualization is possible are the extremists, anarchists. And
depending on what reasons are cited, they are extremists of the right or
left. Again, the unifying factor, and the one of key significance, is the
optimism which the book expresses. Ultimately, I suppose, the attitude
of optimism itself, more than anything else, is the real stranger, a stranger which I make no pretensions whatsoever to grok.

14.

Fritz Leiber and Eyes

JUSTIN LEIBER

Justin Leiber's career is difficult to capsulize, as his achievements are so numerous as to be daunting. He is currently editing a series of historical studies in philosophy and psychology; he has written an impressive number of articles and book reviews with such diverse titles as "Insulting," "Paradigmatic Immorality," "Talking with Extra-Terrestrials," and "Do Apes, Computers, and Humans Have Rights?"; he has published several books, including Noam Chomsky: A Philosophic Overview. *He regularly contributes to the meetings of the American Philosophical Association, and he has taught at six universities, including MIT. He is now associate professor of philosophy at the University of Houston. He has also just finished a science fiction novel,* Beyond Rejection, *that has been made a selection with The Science Fiction Book Club.*

Leiber received his bachelor of philosophy at Oxford, after having received bachelors, masters, and doctorate degrees from the University of Chicago. He has had continued contact with one of the most widely read and respected authors in the science fiction field — his father, Fritz Leiber.

*In this essay, Justin Leiber considers the interplay be-
tween an artist's life and work. A shorter version of this
essay appeared in* Starship: The Magazine about Science Fiction *(formerly* Algol*), vol. 16, no. 3, Summer
1979, pp. 9–20.*

When I talk with philosophers, linguists, and psychologists, I am often struck by the way in which not only the arguments but whole
phrases of their recent writings appear in their conversation. They are,
or become, what they write.

This can be disappointing unless I remind myself that people who
don't write usually have much less to say, and they generally don't
change their patter much from year to year. The barroom remarks
prefaced by "My philosophy of life is . . ." often go decades unrevised.
Boring.

I was first struck by the influence that Fritz's writing had on himself
in the summer of 1968. I had just finished reading Fritz's *A Specter Is
Haunting Texas*, then serialized in *Galaxy Magazine*.

The specter in question is a tall and very thin native of the satellite
communities who must wear a support exoskeleton to visit Texas,
which some two hundred years hence had annexed much of North
America. Scully, an actor by profession, becomes a useful symbolic figure in the Hispanic, "bent-back" revolution against the ruling class of
Texans who use hormones to reach Scully's eight-foot height without
mechanical support.

Science fiction is replete with stories in which the protagonist and a
small band of conspirators try to free "the people" from an evil dictator-
ship. Such stories reveal and reinforce a belief that is common among
science fiction readers: that the character of society is determined by a
technocratic elite. "Revolution" in this view occurs when a good elite,
with fresh intelligence and technology, takes over the dumb masses
and casts out the bad elite.

Scully, to the contrary, is just a co-opted speechmaker, a spectral
mascot. Scully, artist-actor like Fritz, does not change the world—he
reflects it, darkly. (The *Communist Manifesto* begins "A spectre is
haunting Europe, the spectre of Communism . . ." I asked Fritz

whether anyone in science fiction had noticed the source of this title. He said no.)

I hadn't seen Fritz in a couple of years. He had driven in from Los Angeles to do a science fiction writing workshop at Clarion College in Pennsylvania. When I saw Fritz that summer he was sporting all of 140 pounds on his six-foot-five frame—a mighty gaunt reduction from his accustomed 200 or so pounds. He was Scully, or so it seemed to me. He had the silly giddiness of Scully. And he was putting on a crazy dramatic act (at Clarion anyhow). I still have a clear vision of this cadaverous scarecrow capering about and teaching fencing at a drunken backyard party at Clarion. You have to remember that this was the height of the Vietnamese War; LBJ had just withdrawn from running for a second term, which relieved the worries of *Galaxy's* lawyers (*Specter* begins: "Ever since Lyndon ousted Jack in the Early Atomic Age, the term of a President of Texas has been from inauguration to assassination. Murder is merely the continuation of politics by other means.").

You might understand a little of the style of the apparition of Clarion, "Scully" Leiber if you see him striding through that strange film, *Equinox. Equinox* was originally shot with Fritz and four quite amateurish actors and no sound. Later a pro villain, Asmodeus, and sound were added for commercial distribution. Fritz wasn't around at the time to dub. Hence, though you see a lot of him in the film, he says nothing. He just runs endlessly through the underbrush clutching a magic book. (A much younger, handsome, and inexpressive Fritz appears in conversation with Robert Taylor for a second in the Garbo movie *Camille.)*

The same "Scully" version of Fritz turns up in the two other major-award-winning stories of that three-year period, *Ship of Shadows* and *Gonna Roll the Bones.* In *Ship of Shadows* (1969), the protagonist, an ancient and alcoholic floorsweeper of a space bar, shadowboxes his way to reality, sobriety, *and teeth.* (When he visited me in New York City in the spring of 1970, Fritz gave a little talk on his false teeth which I can only describe as brilliant. To speak of such a subject with wit and insight, with careful precision and economy of expression, is characteristic of Fritz. Though he never lost his conversational gifts, his basic diet at that time appeared to be several vitamins and a quart of hard liquor a day.)

In *Gonna Roll the Bones* (1968), one finds recognizable—if myth-proportioned—visions of Fritz, his wife Jonquil, mother Virginia, and the Cat (that is, my father, mother, grandmother, and Gummitch [see "SpaceTime for Springers" for more on the last]). The protagonist, Joe Slattermill, the Quixote of the crap tables of all times and climes from Vicksburg to Vegas, saunters out to shoot dice and comes up against death himself. Fritz drove back to L.A. from Buffalo that summer of 1968 in a Datsun that Jonquil had named "Dunkirk," in honor of the little boats of that desperate evacuation of the British Army from France in the summer of 1940. He stopped in Vegas, and according to one version, had to sell his spare tire for gas to make the last leg into L.A. (See "Night Passage" for a joyful evocation of sexuality and long night drives in the desert after the gambling casinos.)

"Nature imitates Art," as Oscar Wilde put it. Like Joe Slattermill, Fritz won in losing. The last line of *Gonna Roll the Bones* is: "He turned and headed straight for home, but he took the long way, around the world."

In "Waif" (1974) and related stories Fritz does some analysis of his sexuality. Indeed, looking back several decades, Fritz has submerged sexuality in some of his earliest works.

In "Adept's Gambit" (1947 publication, though written several years earlier), we find that grand sword and sorcery pair Fafhrd and Gray Mouser in the ancient Tyre of this world (rather than their now customary world of Nehwon with its adventure, vermin, and vice-infested Lankhmar—that classical medieval port, the one full realization of a city of which we find hints throughout the literature of sword and sorcery). At the center of "Adept's Gambit" is a reclusive, evil young man who experiences the world voyeuristically by sending his sister out under his mental control. Fritz has remarked that he would not have realized at the time he wrote it how much the story suggested about his own sexuality. Fritz, an only child, spent much of his childhood with staid and ancient relatives while his impossibly romantic father and mother toured with his father's Shakespearian repertoire company. He secretly burned the sheets of his first wet dream. It would seem wholly natural that Fritz's first literary mentor was H. P. Lovecraft and that his first stories were supernatural horror. They may have been part of the attempt to revive that quintessentially Victorian sensibility—decadent romanticism—in which the reek of sexuality pervades a landscape of alabaster corpses, little girls in white, unspeakable cellars choked with leprous toadstools, all "splashed with a splendid sickness, the sickness of the pearl" (G. K. Chesterson).

What is extraordinary about Fritz is that he has explored the genre and himself with clarity and determination. In a way, *A Specter Is Haunting Texas* is the supernatural horror story turned inside out: with the specter as point-of-view we get a picaresque farce. Scully is an explicitly sexual specter, brimming with life and fun, revolution and ribaldry. And, above all, Scully is a professional actor (as was Fritz's father) from Circumluna. When he comes to earth for his brief weeks as a specter, the Shakespearian figure is literally true for him: "All the world's a stage."

In "237 Talking Statues" (1963), Fritz makes a kind of amusing peace with his literal father, Fritz Leiber, Sr., or "Guv," as we called him. Guv was a major Shakespearian actor in the 1910s and 1920s. Fritz, under the name "Francis Lathrop," appeared in Guv's repertoire company during its last tour (1934). The Depression meant the end of such companies. Guv's had survived as long as it did because it had a two-year contract with the Chicago Civic Theatre. Fritz now thinks Guv knew the last tour couldn't succeed, but at least father and son would tour together once and it would provide Hollywood exposure. The final tour was planned so that there would be a good run in Los Angeles before the financial collapse. Guv went on to do character roles in the movies and settled into a house in Pacific Palisades. He peopled the Pacific Palisades house with statues and paintings of himself and Virginia (Fritz's mother), usually in Shakespearian roles. Others were represented in less profusion—a statue of me at age four was the major figure in a modest backyard fountain; Fritz displays a bust Guv did of him in the hall of his San Francisco apartment. Guv also liked to paint young women in bathing suits, working from his photographs. The Guv's artwork was what you might expect of a man who also put together a fine darkroom and shop, meticulously maintained and stocked with a very large number of tools, cabinets, and devices that he had made for himself. The kitchen walls, for example, were peopled with nursery-book characters that would gratify a Disney cartoonist in their craftsmanship and unpretension.

In the "237 Talking Statues" we find Francis Legrand II, a mildly alcoholic midlife failure, making his peace with his dead "famous actor" father, who like Guv peopled his home with theatrical self-images. Francis talks to his father, who speaks from one or another of his self-statues, particularly that of Don Juan. Francis speaks of his jealousy and suspicion; his father arranges his own exorcism with affection and dispatch. Mother is persuaded to let one of the cluttering images go. The Don Juan statue is donated to the Merrivale Young Ladies Academy.

The Guv died in 1949. Fritz and Jonquil wound up their Chicago affairs in 1958 and moved to Los Angeles. For a few years they lived in the Pacific Palisades house with Virginia. Then they moved a couple of miles down the coast to Venice, a low-rent hippy-haven with remnants of the canal system that justifies the name. Fritz moved north to San Francisco after Virginia's and finally Jonquil's death in the late 1960s.

Virginia appears, appropriately, as Fafhrd's implacable mother Mor in "The Snow Women" (1970). In some sense she also appears in that story as the eighteen-year-old Fafhrd's first (and last) respectably betrothed Mara. Single and double analogs of Jonquil also appear in the Fafhrd–Gray Mouser saga. But more on that subject later.

Fritz has continued in the "renaissance person" tradition of Guv, though in a more literary, theoretical, and less manual way.

At the University of Chicago Fritz studied psychology and philosophy; there was even a mercifully brief flirtation with religion at the General Theological Seminary in New York City. Fritz is an accomplished fencer. And he is a knowledgeable student of magic, drugs, and psychic powers, though a wholly skeptical one.

Naturally, Fritz is an expert chess player. He won the Santa Monica Open shortly after moving from Chicago to L.A. The *Chess Review* published his version of the *real* first meeting between Sherlock Holmes and Professor Moriarty, "The Moriarty Gambit" (1962). Scene, the first round of the brilliant (and quite real) Hastings International Tournament of 1888. Game, a winning double-rook sacrifice, the most impossibly gaudy of all the grand mating combinations, in which the opponent's Queen is drawn away from the action by the forced "gift" of two rooks, so that the minor pieces may spring a mating net around the opponent's King. The game and players are not recorded in the official records of the Hastings International in the story because both Holmes and Moriarty withdraw from the tournament after the first round.

Fritz is also a great student (professor?) of cities. "Smoke Ghost" (1941) cunningly transforms the "blasted heath" of tradition into the lonely, smoke-ravaged rooftops of warehouses in downtown Chicago. In "Catch That Zeppelin" (1975), we tour Manhattan both in present day and in an alternative world. Fritz can show you what he has deduced to be Sam Spade's movements through the streets of San Francisco in the *Maltese Falcon* just as he has toured so many through the countless byways of mythic Lankhmar. Joanna Russ has her adventurer, Alyx the Picklock, remember having an affectionate brawl with Fafhrd in what must be Lankhmar's Silver Eel. And in Fritz's "The Best Two Thieves in Lankhmar" (1968) Alyx turns up as an observer of Fafhrd's silliness in the back of the same tavern. Fritz's second novel in the "Change War" series is set in late Republican Rome—it has yet to be completed because, according to Fritz, it has become an excuse for reading ever more extensively about the Eternal City. In Fritz's recent novel, *Our Lady of Darkness* (1977), we find "Thibaut de Castries" *Megapolisomancy: A New Science of Cities.*

It is characteristic that Fritz's visual art is minor key. I have a picture over my desk of Frisco's skyline that Fritz did in his spatter-paint technique. When I was a kid "little books," cartoon stories of "Terrinks," "Molly," and "Pommer," appeared on birthdays. Fritz and his friend Harry Fisher (Fafhrd and Gray Mouser) made a Lankhmar game decades ago. The two were recently reunited as guests of honor at a fantasy game convention organized by TSR Games, which now markets a commercial version of Lankhmar.

By far the most valuable device in Fritz's present apartment is a good astronomical telescope. It gets systematic use. Indeed, Fritz's telescopic work helped him discover a tiny degeneration, now successfully laser-arrested, in one retina. Since you look through a telescope with only one eye, such damage can be detected early. Fritz's first thought was that there was something amiss with the telescope; then he worked back to the eye. Outward vision is inward vision: "He headed straight for home, but he took the long way, around the world." This incident is the theme of this essay in a minor variation. Fritz found what was amiss in himself in his art.

Recently, Fritz showed me a short piece that recounts his examination of his cheap but functional, hour-minute, digital-display, electric clock. The prose is a model of clarity and concision, an exercise in observation, deduction, discovery, and more deduction, that is a miniature, a bit of Cellini goldwork, of disciplined thought and investigation. The final discovery that the clock has a sixty-seven-second minute and a correlative fifty-three-second minute in each hour is reached through a series of observations and deductions that give us a sharp picture of what ought to happen when one thinks about the discontinuities between the physical features of machines and the rather different cognitive functions—such as giving the correct time—that we want them to exhibit.

What makes this intellectual paradigm so interesting is that it maps a territory that is characteristic of the best of recent work in human cognitive psychology. Fritz read my article, "Extraterrestrial Translation" (*Galileo* 7, 1978) and part of my *Structuralism* (G. K. Hall, 1978), in which I write as a professional philosopher about cognitive psychology. Then he handed me his piece about his electric clock. *Padre, padrone:* father, master. Perhaps it's a comfort that Fritz mentioned that when he was taught to play chess, Guv decided that he wanted to learn too; Guv beat the kid. Grand-*padre*, grand-*padrone*.

Fritz was an editor of *Science Digest* from 1945 to 1957. Particularly during that period he produced many articles on scientific subjects. One standard family activity of the late 1940s, when I was about nine years old, was the old collation march around the dining room table, assembling copies of *New Purposes*, a mimeo magazine that Fritz got out, with a little help from his friends—and for his friends.

Reflecting on that period in my own life, I am struck by the degree to which I was being shown the future. When Marshall McLuhan danced into the cultural gestalt in the middle 1960s, I was able to yawn. McLuhan's first book, *The Mechanical Bride*, appeared at home shortly after its publication in 1951. It contained a substantial analysis of Fritz's "The Girl with the Hungry Eyes" (1949). *The Mechanical Bride* had the standard McLuhan scam: it fell "stillborn from the press" because the audience was out of phase.

Fritz is above all prodigal in the variety of literary forms he has employed — and invented: poetry from sonnets through the varieties of more gaudy meters, ten-page letter correspondences in the pre-twentieth-century manner, short stories written to fit magazine covers, essays on social questions, short plays, songs and chants, parodies of Robert Heinlein and Micky Spillane, historical and crime tales, a still-to-be-completed book on the fantasy novel, and so on.

What is striking is the degree to which much of this is motivated by friendship and the challenge of yet another form. *Sonnets for Jonquil*, a blue-covered mimeo, contains some of Jonquil's poetry and a note on her other writing, including a play that Fritz helped put on, plus some sonnets by Fritz about Jonquil.

"The Lords of Quarmall" (1964) bears the note, "In 1936 my comrade Harry Otto Fischer conceived, began, and abandoned the story 'The Lords of Quarmall.' Twenty-five years later I decided I was up to the pleasant task of solving the mysteries of the tale and completing it without changing his words at all, except to add details of the plot. Harry, in some ways a very patient person, laconically commented that he was glad to discover at last how his story ended." If you read that story, which appears in the fourth Fafhrd–Gray Mouser book, and distinguish Harry's passages from the story that Fritz wove around them, you will have a curious lesson in comradeship.

(Oh dear, have I forgotten to mention the stories and novels that have won Fritz more professional [Nebula] and fan [Hugo] awards than any other writer? And the fact that in 1979 he became the only writer except Heinlein to have twice been the exclusive guest of honor at the World Science Fiction Convention? Ah, but that's the point. Though Fritz presents himself as a freelance writer by trade, with no high art pretentions, there is simply no one in science fiction with anything remotely like his prestige or talent who shows less of an interest in the big money or is more of a soft touch for "fanzine" editors who beg for a piece to give their amateur magazines some class. Fritz simply likes to write a lot of different kinds of things, and if half of them are ahead of their time or behind their time or so far out in left field that the people who have the right background to read them can be counted on your fingers—well, tough. "The Moriarty Gambit," for example, calls for a reader who likes to play out others' games from chess notation and who knows the Sherlock Holmes stories and is crazy about them.)

But since Fritz is known for his award-winning science fiction writing, I want to say a little about one of his most original and form-forging works, *The Big Time*. *The Big Time* introduces the "Change War" world, in which a vast war is conducted through space and time by "Spiders" and "Snakes," and by humans and extraterrestrials who have the flexibility and alienation that allow them to be drawn away from their ordinary lives and into the big time, the world of all times and possibilities.

Many time travel stories suggest that one might travel to the Ice Age, mash a blade of grass, and change all history. But if you think about it, if time travel is possible then all of time must exist at once in some sense—the past cannot have wholly disappeared if you can get to it, nor can the future be wholly unmade if you can go there and back. This raises the question as to how one can change the future or the past. This also raises another question: what is the present? If you can travel the big time continuum of space-time-history from ancient Egypt to the distant future, who is to say what slice is the present?

Strikingly, Fritz has an elegant answer to these questions—the "law of the conservation of reality." The idea is to extend the conservation laws of physics once more, into the psychological, historical, and higher physical sciences. As you know, two conservation laws were the hallmarks of eighteenth- and nineteenth-century science: (1) mass (matter) is neither created nor destroyed, though it may change form from a liquid to a gas, enter into a chemical reaction, and so on; and (2) energy is neither created nor destroyed, though it can change from random heat to mechanical motion, sound, ranges in the electro-magnetic spectrum, and so on.

These conservation laws generalize cruder and more specific conservations and they have been generalized themselves in this century. We now have, as Einstein's $E = MC^2$ suggests, the law of the conservation of mass energy: the total amount of mass energy is conserved, though you can transform one into the other as stars do all the time. (The powerful grip of this conservation law today is suggested by the fact that scientists have been much more willing to accept the notion that the universe had a "big bang" beginning in time, which is disturbing enough, than the sort of "steady state" theory which requires the spontaneous addition of new mass energy continuously.)

The law of the conservation of reality, like the other conservation laws, suggests that nothing is really lost, nothing spontaneously evaporates or appears. You can, with a great expenditure of reality through time travel agents, transform something in the space-time-history continuum (replace Julius Caesar with a secret Spider agent, throw a tactical A-bomb into the Peloponnesian War), *but the rest of the historical continuum will conserve reality.* It will change the absolute minimum needed to accommodate this intervention.

In another Change War story, a big time recruit goes back to prevent his being shot in ordinary time, altering as little as possible so that no bullet hits him. Nature makes the proper hole in him with a meteor just as the bullet would. This mere improbability is the most conservative step nature can take in changing the continuum of history and its generalization and laws. *Something* has to be done so that ordinary time t_1, in which X has no hole in his head, is going to fit smoothly with ordinary time t_2, in which X has a hole, and in which many other events seem to occur in consequence of this hole and its being very much like a bullet hole. Time travel in ordinary time violates reality; reality reshapes the pattern of events so that the violation fits right in with a new reality of ordinary time. (In still another Change War short story, we have a brief view of the real Shakespeare—that is, the person who was Shakespeare before the Snakes and Spiders started messing about—suffering through a viewing of a performance of Duff Beth, a play that the real Shakespeare had growing within him.)

What is the present in the continuum of ordinary time? The present is simply the slice of history that is most conserved, least changeable, most influential.

Formally, *The Big Time* maintains the most strict unities of classical drama. The entire story takes place within a few hours and in one large room, a rest and recreation station outside of time. The Cast—the Place is obviously a theatre and the action dramatic—composed of entertainers and agents, comes from choice points in history, or slightly altered, "Change War torn" history. This provides the challenge of displaying very different accents and modes of thought together. The Place is like a ghostly theatre in which characters from different plays meet. Take Karysia Labrys, originally of the ancient Crete of the Triple-Goddess, who gives the following description of the battle she has just returned from with a Lunan and a satyr:

Woe to Spider! Woe to Cretan! Heavy is the news I bring you. Bear it bravely like strong women. When we got the gun unlimbered, I heard seaweed fry and crackle. We three leaped behind the rock wall, saw our guns grow white as sunlight in a heat-ray of the Serpents! Natch, we feared we were outnumbered and I called upon my Caller. . . .

But I didn't die there, kiddos. I still hoped to hurt the Greek ships, maybe with the Snake's own heat gun. So I quick tried to outflank them. My two comrades crawled beside me—they are males but they have courage. Soon we spied the ambushsetters. They were Snakes and they were many, filthily disguised as Cretans. . . .

They had seen us when we saw them, and they loosed a killing volley. Heat- and knife-rays struck about us in a storm of wind and fire, and the Lunan lost a feeler, fighting for Crete's Triple Goddess. So we dodged behind a sand hill, steered our flight back toward the water. It was awful, what we saw there; Crete's brave ships all sunk or sinking, blue sky sullied by their death-smoke. Once again the Greeks had licked us!—aided by the filthy Serpents. Round our wrecks, their black ships scurried, like black beetles, filth their diet, yet this day they dine on heroes. On the quiet sun-lit beach there, I could feel a Change Gale blowing, working changes deep inside me, aches and pains that were a stranger's. Half my memories were doubled, half my lifeline crooked and twisted, three new moles upon my swordhand. Goddess, Goddess, Triple Goddess . . . Triple Goddess, give me courage to tell all that happened.

Let's suppose you did recruit such a fighter and equipped her with ordinary English rather than the stilted language that scholars will

likely use when they translate a popular, preliterate folk epic poem like
the *Iliad*. If you didn't notice the rhythm in Kaby's chant, read it aloud.
But also note the fierce feminism of Kaby. Joanna Russ's Alyx is much
like her, particularly in *Picnic in Paradise* (1968), and Russ's work is recognized, correctly, as the first real entry of feminism in science fiction.
But Fritz thought up Kaby in 1958.

I could make similar points about the rest of the cast. The narrator-
entertainer, Greta Forzane of Depression Chicago, Prussian Erich von
Hohenwald, WWI poet-soldier Bruce Marchant, riverboat gambler
Beau, Doc of Nazi-occupied Tzarist Russia, Sidney Lessingham of
sixteenth-century London, and so on. The plot and action form a
tightly-structured roller coaster that leaves you breathless. But the
Lunan Illilihis provides the final revelation, slid in so casually that I
missed it until this last reading:

> Feeling sad, Greta girl, because you'll never understand what's happen-
> ing to us all, because you'll never be anything but a shadow fighting
> shadows. . . . Who are the real Spiders and Snakes, meaning who were
> the first possibility-binders? Who was Adam? Lilith? In binding all possi-
> bility, the Demons also bind the mental with the material. All fourth-
> order beings live inside and outside all minds, throughout the whole
> cosmos. Even this place is, after all its fashion, a giant brain: its floor is
> the brain-pan, the boundary of the Void is the cortex of gray matter—
> yes even the Major and Minor Maintainers are analogues of the pineal
> and pituitary glands, which in some form sustain all nervous systems.

The mind is really the big time. For we find there a constructed reality, a panorama of space-time-history that flexes and readjusts as one
reconstructs the past and repredicts the future, reintegrates the macro-
cosm and microcosm. At the same time, in the mind's big time, there is
the continual play of possibilities, of alternate histories and worlds.
The cast of the Place worry that the Snakes and Spiders may have
messed so much with the fabric of historical reality that it may fission,
smashing the conservation of matter. But that's what madness is, isn't
it? The Ego can put it together no longer.

You will also notice in *The Big Time* a view of the mind that is as old
as Plato and as new as Hermann Hesse's *Steppenwolf:* the mind is com-

posed of many persons, forged in fear and love, from experience, history, and imagination; and when the mind acts or receives reports, it does so through one or another of these characters and must take account of that character's weaknesses.

In one of his brilliant philosophical puzzle pieces Jorge Borges has Shakespeare wonder that he has no "real me" inside but rather a vast cast, he is "everyone or no one." Borges' story concludes when God tells Shakespeare that he feels the same way. In another short story, "Borges and I," Borges, comparing his inner sense of self with the construction that is reflected by the body of his writings, concludes that "I do not know which of us is writing this line." But all of this is simply more true of a writer than of most of us.

Borges' Shakespearian commentary summarizes a theory of the turn-of-the-century French philosopher Henri Bergson about the difference between tragic and comic literature. Bergson proposed that major tragic characters are versions of the author's self. Thus Bergson suggests that Hamlet and MacBeth are Shakespeare, or what he might have been in particular circumstances.

Hence, expanding on Bergson: (1) Tragic high art is, consciously or unconsciously, a confession by the author. It is about the author's selves (not about "self" because there are many, not "his" or "her" because the author is male and female, even nonhuman, by turns); and (2) Since the author is, above all, an author, a maker and creator, tragic high art is about itself, about creation and illusion, about the selves and sanity, about the differences (or lack of them) between the "real" world and the reflections and extrapolations of it that authors make. (But remember that in creating worlds, the artist is doing what every mind does in trying to put together a realistic picture of the world outside, and since that world outside has no view or picture, realistic or unrealistic, true or false, about itself, appearance may be the only reality, and artistic creations the purest and most honest world-making.)

My third point about Bergson's theory seems to follow from the other two, from the point that tragic high art is a confession of the author's inner selves, and the point that such art is about itself. "Borges and I" suggests the paradox that follows—the underlying source of the goosebumps that high art causes. The third point is that an author gradually puts together a picture of himself or herself through works authored. Usually the picture is created indirectly and inadvertently. We know the author through his attitudes and perceptions that have created this cast of characters, that has them do these things and suffer these fates, and sets them into this or that reality. These works reflect, give birth to, an author in a much fuller sense than that a distortion in the sky may suggest a degeneration in the retina of the viewing eye. The more narrow and rigid the genre, and the more impersonal, limited, or technically-demanding its style or meter, the more subtle (provided the work is skillful) will the reflected author appear.

In his initial choice of supernatural horror and sword and sorcery genres, shy Fritz would seem to have found just what he needed to lose himself in. These are pulp, lowbrow genres—no pretension in that. They impose on those who write them a colorful and gaudy vocabulary and style; they also impose a special sort of atmosphere, landscape, and arcane lore. Excepting science fiction, they are alone among pulp forms in combining brawny, physical combat with the cut and thrust of intelligence.

Finally, these forms dictate clever, gimicky plot construction and rapid action; even the emotional punch is much restricted. One can write recipes for these genres, and people do. It seems to follow that one reveals nothing about oneself in this type of writing except that one knows the recipe and can follow directions. Further, because these are both physical and minor genres, to write them reveals no pretensions to high art or fair fame. Rather, they generate a relatively small circle of initiates and playful semiprofessionals. Perhaps in this cozy circle Fritz found something of a replacement for "the company," his father's Shakespearian band.

Indeed, Shakespeare himself was both a "humble player" of a popular art and archmage of an arcane fellowship, and his plays continually reverberate with this. He was not only his characters in that they were people he might have been, but, as Bergson suggests, Shakespeare also played these roles on stage. Shakespearian actors take particular relish in those "humble player" speeches which suggest that one is playing Shakespeare himself acting the part of a "humble player," who in turn is playing a particular role. Not only did Shakespeare create his actors and their ethos as the flip side of the onstage characters, but he made it easy for the traditional Shakespearian actor to hallow deep within the conviction that "I am Shakespeare."

Perhaps Fritz should have been more wary. If the play, occasionally, is the thing to catch the conscience of the king, it is always ready to cast murky, indirect, and devastating reflections of the playwright. The Shakespearian actor does not run that risk of looking through a telescope at a strange and entrancing world only to find a terrifying reflection of the actor's self. The view that high art is confessional and consciously self-reflective suggests not only that it may be therapeutic but also that it is dangerous and painful.

It is interesting that we here find a parallel to magic, or at least to what is said about magic in Eddison's definitive *The Worm Oroboros*, one of Fritz's favorite books: the more powerful the magical effects one wants, the more the effort and danger in conjuring, the more the conjuror is likely to suffer a reflection of what is intended for the victim.

Recalling the telescope analogy, these points seem to follow happily: (1) The better and more self-conscious the artist's choice and use of tools, of words and scene construction, the more likely that the dangerous inner vision will result, though the casual reader may merely feel the hair rise on the back of the neck and not know why. The more accurate and powerful the telescope, the more the observer knows and cares about the capacities and limitations of it and the more likely the observer will be able to reach interesting and precise insights. The more self-conscious and precise one is about language and plot, the more likely one will pick up the ghostly reflections of other alien influences. (2) Similarly, the more the artist knows about characters and worlds, and the more coherent and detailed the artistic visions, the more likely the artist will notice alien distortions. At this point, we have the beginning of the Borges' doubling in "Borges and I": there is now the other Borges, the ever-growing persona that the published works reflect, and as ever the inner I. High art encompasses more and more of the author because it is forced to, as the Ego's logic forces it to displace Id, as the public Borges replaces his I. Any dream may realize it has a dreamer, but then the dreamer becomes a part of the dream, and the dream acquires another level of structure. But the dream that this sort of dreamer dreams is itself a still greater dream and so must have still another dreamer, and so on. High art plays endlessly on this paradox and its analogs. Like Eddison's *Worm*, it is always swallowing its own tale/tail.

That is why the artist is neither simply escaping into dreamland nor engaged in self-analytic therapy. Of course, Fritz undoubtedly got simple pleasure from picturing the sword and sorcery world of Lankhmar, from making a barbarian adventurer Fafhrd that had his height and none of his self-consciousness.

But the artist, of course, has a craft and is trying to tell a story to someone else. Even if the artist starts with a simple, wish-fulfilling cast and dream, the artist is driven to make the dream more dazzling, compelling, and seductive. The wish-fulfillment may be made more complete and less obvious to the reader—the artist is always forced to understand the magic of the machinery, with which the reader is bewitched.

But the artist isn't seeking self-therapy either, though that is a byproduct. That is the disanalogy with the telescope incident. When Fritz noticed something in the heavens that couldn't be there, he checked the telescope, and finally worked back to the damage in his eye. Then, naturally, he got medical treatment.

It is true, and it is part of my thesis, that Fritz started with escapist and deliberately unpretentious genres—Id demanded gross meals, and shyness (murderous Superego) insisted on concealment in pulp genre—but, as Fritz improved his art and grasp of form, his artistic daemon, reflecting on past work and planning new simply forced him to realize various pathologies in himself, forced him into better self-understanding. When the Id demands skillful pornography from the Ego's endless spinning of wispy webs, it should watch out, for it may find by some sudden slight that it is not the king speaking to a humble player but the bull facing the matador.

But art is neither astronomy nor therapy. We are neither trying to free from distortion our observation of a real world up there, nor using aberrations in reports of some arbitrary phenomenon like inkblots are used to diagnose pathologies. The artist creates a world with its creator included—a tale that includes its own telling and feeds upon itself. The play's the thing, not the player. Art is not a caricature of dream or dream analysis: they are caricatures, degradations, of art, just as Freud explicitly maintained that paranoia is a caricature of philosophy, and compulsion neurosis a caricature of religion. Art creates worlds that are real and valuable, rather than fog on the lens, pathologic and diagnostic. The artist is like the psychologist, not the patient, and the artist aims at truth and not comfort, at wonder and not relaxation.

Therapy is a caricature of high art because the therapist must believe, in guiding the patient toward self-knowledge, that this self–knowledge will lead to a remission of the patient's symptoms, of the fears and pains the patient wished to have removed in therapy. The therapist will not feel very unhappy if the patient's "self-knowledge" proves to be neither very knowing nor very accurate if the patient's symptoms go away. Nor will the therapist feel justified in continuing a course of therapy that seems to give the patient a more and more accurate and insightful knowledge of self, while this very self-knowledge makes the patient increasingly nervous, unhappy, or suicidal.

On the other hand, if we have a teacher and a student, artist and audience, scientist and colleague, we will care more about understanding and worry very little about pathological reactions. We have the closest to art in the following case: Freud writes of his own self-analysis for an audience of psychologists and the general public—but Freud's intent is truth first, education second, and general excitement third.

Speaking in the therapeutic, caricaturist mode, Freud gives us a myth of the human mind in which reason and creativity (Ego) rationalize, shamming up whatever fantasy-world that can satisfy the rude demands of kind Id without offending archbishop Superego. Speaking in the artistic and creative mode, Plato gives us in the *Republic* what Freud caricatures: inside us there is a man, a lion, and a ravenous monster; under proper conditions the man, which is to say reason and creativity, runs matters, schooling lion and monster to run in tandem. But of course the man inside that Plato speaks of *is* Reason and Art, struggling out of a fleshy cocoon. Art and Science, just as Reason itself, have this way with flesh: the mortal Einstein was Einstein's theory's way of creating itself just as poor mortal William, long dead globe actor, was Shakespeare's way of creating itself.

Illy, the Lunan of *The Big Time* who hints that the Place and its Cast are a mind, also remarks,

> Remember that the Serpent is your symbol of wisdom and the Spider your sign of patience: the two are rightly frightening to you, for all high existence is a mixture of horror and delight.

Fritz soon grew unchallenged by the supernatural horror and sword and sorcery forms with which he began. Once one gives oneself to art one may become discontent with simple tasks and low dreams. His first substantial works are rich in ideas and technologies, though retaining much of the atmosphere of the earlier tales. The unpretentious pose of the professional pulp writer is maintained. The ideas and characters are there to wring the maximum punch from the dramatic, swift-moving action that clever plotting affords; style and narrative structure are unobtrusive. The protagonist is invariably an attractive and uncomplicated character with whom the reader may easily identify, both innocently awaiting the tricks that are in store. Though the protagonist often shares a couple of skills or experiences with the real Fritz — surely the writer has to know something about the settings he puts his characters into — the protagonist is no confession of the real Fritz, nor is there any tricky interplay between protagonist and artist.

All this begins to turn around in the later works: *You're All Alone, Gather Darkness,* and *Conjure Wife* of the 1940s, followed by *The Big Time, Specter,* and *Our Lady of Darkness.*

In *You're All Alone* (1950) one of the narrowest and most dramatic expressions of paranoia that I have known is explored. The protagonist discovers that almost everyone in his present-day world operates like a Leibnizian "windowless" monad. They all are following a prearranged, automatic pattern that makes them look like they are interacting while in fact they are not. If you are one of the very few who can break out of the pattern, no one will notice you. And indeed they all continue "interacting" with the empty space you are programmed to occupy exactly as if you were there. The "all" does not include a small number of evil breakouts who are exploiting the situation and hunting down everyone else who has broken out of the automatic interplay. Eerie effects come from manipulation of the automaton normals, from retreating to the automatic patterns.

It's a scarey story, and should one stand back and think about it, it suggests something about the writer (about a grim Chicago downtown business-and-bar world). But everything is done to lead the reader away from that issue, and the author has no place in the story. The title is "You're All Alone," not "I'm All Alone" or "We're All Alone."

On the other hand, *The Big Time* employs the same notion of breakout for the few whom the Snakes and Spiders can recruit. They do not break out of themselves, however, and Illy eventually suggests that the recruiter is really the demon-daemon Art. Here we have not the simple paranoiac punch but the gay, giddy, multileveled fabric of high art, of the "everybody and nobody," in which the Place, dancing with drama and history, is also revealed as the mind of Fritz Leiber and his Art (like "I" and "Borges").

Gather Darkness (1943) is one of the first (perhaps *the*) classical novels of a future, post-World War Three world dominated by an authoritarian, medieval church hierarchy whose inner circle employs a secret scientific technology to keep a superstitious public and lower priesthood under control. The action is dramatic and colorful, the technology cunning and charming, the plot stunningly well constructed. One idea that gives the work its classical balance is the logic of a revolution against such a hierarchy of white magic. The revolutionaries will play satanists, a hierarchy of black magic which will dismay, frighten, or win over people who are accustomed to thinking in magical, not scientific ways. (The French historian, Jules Michelet, saw medieval satanism as the only available expression for the antifeudal revolution. If the church hierarchy says that God wants all wealth and power to go to the temporal and religious lords, who is on the side of the poor peasants? Who is their spiritual resource?)

But, as I've suggested, when we get to *A Specter Is Haunting Texas* (1968), we have a more multileveled, more comic and realistic story of a post-World War Three future. Scully, actor from Circumluna, is dragged into the Hispanic revolution against hormone-hiked, conquering Texans, who identify the LBJ and (no doubt) a certain war. And Scully knows that history is seldom a tale of technologically inventive elites, coldly manipulating the credulous masses. You don't reason its craziness out, you sing it, chant it, farce it out.

In *Conjure Wife* (1943) we have what Damon Knight insisted was the "necessarily-definitive" tale of witchcraft. The protagonist, Norman Saylor, teaches anthropology at a small college. One day he discovers that his wife Tansy is practicing witchcraft. She reluctantly admits that she thinks she is protecting them with various devices; still more reluctantly she is persuaded to give up her superstitions, to discard her protectors. Naturally, strange and increasingly harmful events begin to multiply; disaster looms around them, eventually taking Tansy's soul. Norman's intelligence finally forces him to give up skepticism and to use symbolic logic from hints and variations in magic books in an attempt to derive the "ur-formula" that will return Tansy. Tansy was, of course, defending Norman from the witchcraft of the female faculty members and faculty wives. (Catch the English version of the novel on the late show under the title, *Burn, Witch, Burn.*)

It is true that Fritz had a brief teaching post at Occidental College and that Jonquil then, as always, had a fascination with witchcraft and had read much about it. On the other hand, Fritz taught drama and stagecraft. And Norman is the familiar neutral protagonist of this period. He is no real confession of Fritz. And Fritz has never been converted to a belief in the supernatural. *Conjure Wife* is Fritz's first published novel, and he did not return to the novel of magic until his latest, *Our Lady of Darkness.*

This latest novel plays upon a theme to which Borges has brought our attention, something that Thomas Pynchon's work typifies: the pollution of reality by dream—or dream by reality, for the pollution is the trickery of mirrors and artistic representation.

The protagonist of *Our Lady of Darkness* is a writer of horror stories, Franz Weston, who just happens to live at 811 Geary Street in San Francisco, and has a landlady and some friends who happen to have the same names and personalities as the friends of Fritz Leiber of 811 Geary Street. Similarly, the engine of horror draws from the activities of various people in the first decades of the century, some real, some partly real, so cunningly intertwined that the reader cannot see the seams. And the final tip of the engine that most closely attacks Franz is his "scholar's mistress," the pile of pulp novels and source books that share Franz's bed, for he lives in one room and often writes in bed.

Thiabaut de Castries, decades-dead author of *Megapolisomancy: A New Science of Cities*, who is the possible ultimate source of this attack, says of another book of his that is originally aimed at (the real) Clark Ashton Smith, "Go out, my little book, into the world, and lie in wait in stalls and lurk on shelves for the unwary purchaser. Go out, my little book, and break some necks!"

As Fritz's art has developed it becomes ever more willing to play and joke, to fool with words and themes, to inject comic gaiety into the midst of tragedy. My favorite in the pure comic vein is "Mysterious Doings in the Metropolitan Museum" (1974), a tale of insect political conventioneering.

If my theme is that Fritz's art progressed in his growth in self-knowledge, what am I to do with the claim that Bergson paired with his view that the tragedian writes about possible selves of the tragedian? Let me reply to this objection. Bergson also claimed that the comedian writes not about the comedian's inner selves but about social types (class abstracts so to speak). But it is obvious that mad, death-defying gaiety, black comedy, is central to the most important fiction in our century (James Joyce, John Barth, André Gide, Nathaniel West, and so on). So let me just say that if, as in *The Big Time*, you realize that a so-called individual mind is really a composition of characters, more or less stereotyped and capable of independent action, then you realize that Plato was right in having Socrates insist in the *Symposium* that the art of the comedian is the same as that of the tragedian. Of course, Plato's *Symposium* is narrated by a youth who becomes sufficiently intoxicated so that he falls asleep after hearing the speeches, only awakening at dawn to hear Socrates' conclusion and not his argument—tricky characters, these poet-philosophers.

I have suggested that as Fritz's art developed he came to employ richer and more complicated forms, came to use himself and his artistic self-image in his art, came to play the mirror tricks of high art. But one might argue that this doesn't fit the Fafhrd–Gray Mouser stories with which Fritz began and which he has continued throughout his career. Surely, Fafhrd is a vision of Fritz himself, or so someone might object.

Well, I certainly have to admit that when I was a kid both my mother Jonquil and I called Fritz "Faf" or "Fafhrd" more than anything else. And it is true that both Fafhrd and Fritz share impressive height and a taste for strong drink and songs. And in 1943 Harry Fisher wrote Fritz a long letter in which he briefly mentioned a Gray Mouser who "walks with swagger 'mongst the bravos, though he's but the stature of a child," and a tall barbarian Fafhrd whose "wrist between gauntlet and mail was white as milk and thick as a heroe's ankle."

But one is skeptical, particularly considering the shyness with which Fritz started and his admissions that he felt, initially, overwhelmed by young Harry and prepared to learn from him. After all, it's Harry that provides the initial description. Gray Mouser fits Harry's vision of himself as Loki-like trickster, skilled swordsman, wit, and dabbler in dark lore, the footloose adventurer and gentleman thief, onliest companion of the "seven-foot" barbarian Fafhrd.

Given just this pairing of city cat cunning and barbarian bear, and a certain humility coupled with a sense of story, it seems natural that Fritz's first Fafhrd–Gray Mouser stories should have been written from the Mouser viewpoint. In many of these stories, cunning and feline Mouser saves the honest, unsophisticated barbarian giant from the sort of bewitchment or other exotic danger that the blockhead would walk into. You can't have the tall barbarian saving the tiny Mouser, for there is no balance of amusing inversion in that. Fafhrd is the natural straight man, the butt of the jest.

And since sword and sorcery adventures are not read by swordsmen or confident, brawny brawlers, rather attracting bookish and brainy types who just fancy physical adventure, it is natural that the audience is attracted to Gray Mouser and his slippery victories over the big brawlers. (It belongs to the high comedy of art and life that when Fritz and Harry recently surfaced publicly as Fafhrd and Gray Mouser at the TRS game convention, Fritz should have felt uneasy until he realized that, as Gray Mouser, Harry was attracting more attention and dominating matters, with Fritz suffering as Fafhrd rather than the author of the imaginary world. This is a second minor variation of the theme, a complement to the telescope story.)

So I am inclined to think that Fritz wasn't Fafhrd from the beginning, though—and this is the rest of my reply—Fafhrd eventually becomes more Fritz-like. Certainly, there are some revealing and confessional changes as the saga develops.

The first tales are quest stories in which the twain are lured into some doomful quest, drawn and nearly overwhelmed by some distant and lonely horror. The atmosphere is a relatively uniform feeling of somber eeriness, mounting to a chilling climax.

In the latter stories Fritz has a much surer and broader sense of language and plot. Comedy and gaiety invade the saga, romance and drunken silliness appear, and grand Lankhmar becomes central with its motley of religions, beggars' and thieves' guilds, necromancers and decadent aristocrats, gates and streets, mysterious houses and musty passages, shops and taverns, gods and humanlike animals.

My favorite is "Lean Times in Lankhmar," in which the penniless and disaffected twain separate. Mouser hires himself out as a protection racket enforcer, covering the religions that move up the Street of the Gods as they attract a following and down as they lose it. Fafhrd becomes an acolyte of Issek of the Jug, swearing off booze and swords. The confrontation that must occur as Issek of the Jug moves up to the successful part of the street is managed with such astonishing deftness, twist upon twist, that one finds oneself laughing "too much, too much," only to have yet another carefully prepared rabbit pop out of that hat, and yet another after that. The story plays effortlessly with the inversions of high art.

Fritz (and reality) seep into the saga world. Fritz has some fairly somber things to say about hard drinking that point much more to Fritz than to the Fafhrd of the very first stories. And, as I remarked some pages back, various family figures appear.

In the most recent novel, *Rime Isle* (1977), in the second half of the sixth volume, *Swords and Ice Magic*, a considerable further step is taken. Fafhrd and Mouser are hired by two women councillors of Rime Isle, an atheistic and practical fishing community which is thereby somewhat estranged from the Lankhmar world and on the border of others. Fafhrd arrives with a ship and a small band of well-trained berserkers, and Mouser with a crew of Mingols and a band of disciplined Lankhmar thieves.

The story has begun some time earlier when very faint versions of Loki and Odin had appeared from another world and were gradually nurtured into somewhat more palpable existence by the councillors Afreyt and Cif. The gods Loki and Odin insisted that Rime Isle is threatened by hordes of Mingols, inspired by another deity.

Gradually, as defenses are prepared, it becomes clear that tricky Loki really intends a sea disaster in which all sides are destroyed and, even more clearly, Odin wants to see as many participants as possible killed in a land battle, with the remainder hanged. Young Fritz found the Bulfinch picture of the Norse gods attractive, particularly of the mysterious and wise Odin. More recent research has made it clear that Odin was the center of a death cult. Here on Rime Isle Odin insists that his followers wear hangman nooses and carry a gallows into battle. Fafhrd, apparently less affected by Odin's wiles, refuses to wear his noose around his neck but places it around his left wrist as a concession.

At the last moment both Mouser, who is directing the sea forces, and Fafhrd, on land, throw off the bewitchments of trickery and death. Neither their own men and the Rime Islers nor their similarly inspired opponents are drawn into the grand doom that the gods intend. All part somewhat dazed, except that the noose around Fafhrd's hand draws tight and that famous bravo, now responsible protector of a practical and atheistic community, has no left hand.

To my questioning statement, "Conan Doyle unsuccessfully killed off Sherlock Holmes but at least he didn't maim him," Fritz rather tersely replied that it just seemed to him that no one was really getting hurt in the story. Ah yes, old trickster—but what does Prospero say on that island when he abjures his powerful magic, remembering that he is traditionally regarded as Shakespeare's mouthpiece?—"I'll break my staff, bury it certain fathoms in the earth, and deeper than did ever plummet sound I'll drown my book."

To be sure, *Rime Isle* is even more comparable to Goethe's *Faust II*, in which Faust abjures the pursuit of esoteric knowledge and immortality, the deals with tricky Mephistofeles, in order to help a small island community develop a healthy and happy life. Through history, the left hand has been the symbol of trickiness and death; we now know it as the hand of the right brain, which may be full of visions but has not the words and reason of the left brain which controls the right (the writing) hand. That last point may even suggest that nature has a taste for the inversions of high art. Who knows what tales tell us?

Fritz Leiber assumes humility in writing or speaking of his own art. He will say that all he has ever wanted to do is tell a good story. His works, Borges-Shakespeare style, conceal and jest with their structures. How am I to reply?

In the "Moriarty Gambit" Fritz makes a solid point in distinguishing the real Sherlock Holmes from the "thinking machine" carefully analyzed by Watson in that first great novel, *A Study in Scarlet*. Watson, wondering what his newly acquired roommate's profession is, lists the kinds of knowledge Holmes possesses. Watson's list, though Watson does not draw this inference, suggests that Holmes has systematically stocked his mind with what a detective might need, and, just as systematically, has not stocked it with irrelevant information. (Watson is shocked that Holmes does not know that the earth orbits the sun.)

Fritz points out that as one reads the stories it becomes clear that Holmes knows almost everything there is to be known—it is natural that he should play expert chess, though Conan Doyle fails to mention it. Well-made characters have an integrity that gives them dimensions outside what their written stories tell us, and certainly outside or even opposing what their authors explicitly state about them.

That high art should be about itself seems overly pretentious. There is absolutely nothing more familiar and pedestrian than the complaint that supposed "mainstream," "serious" novels are often written by academics to be read and studied by professors and graduate students. But surely nothing is more characteristic of profession, craft, skill, and artistry than an interest in impressing aficionados. Even TV ads often work hard to attain a quality of verve and elegance, of artistry extravagantly yoked to other ends, quite beyond any pragmatic concern with mass sales. The same case can be made of Renaissance church art. A professional writer writes about vocations, undertaking, and locales that are familiar to him or her. If he or she knows how hospitals work, by all means he or she should set a story there. Dashiel Hammett had been a detective. Yet what is more familiar to a writer than writing, than himself?

I have suggested that in the punning play, paradox, and self-swallowing of high art there is important truth. But why the Borges-Shakespearian paradoxical way? Why not blunt truth? Or complicated truth straightforwardly presented?

I have mentioned Plato as an example of such play in philosophy. But perhaps a more modern argument might be extracted. Bertrand Russell said that a philosopher-logician should be ever on the lookout for paradoxes, for they will be the best source for getting at the hidden structure of our language and thought. He had in mind sentences such as the next one in this paragraph. This sentence is false. (But of course if the sentence indeed is false, then it must be true because that's what it says; but if it is true, then it is false because . . .) But that sentence is also like a work of art: it tells no literal facts but it teaches much if one is attentive. And it surely, like the worm Oroboros, swallows its own tale/tail.

One can say this neurobiologically—art above all recreates and educates our cognitive abilities, sharpens our ears and eyes, tunes our understanding and sensitivity. It serves for us something like the function of play among mammals such as the cats. We get by with our intellect and sensitivities. Art recreates them. Cats get by with their agility and claws. Play exercises these strengths. Language is the human mind's oldest technology and most basic extraordinary cognitive capacity. So the kind of art that most sensitizes us to language—that is to logic and meter, to writing and artistic form, to the interplay between language and reality—is the art that appeals to our oldest, most powerful and most central faculty, housed in our left brain, a blend of artifact and neurology that has made us different from the other mammals.

Fritz combines an awesome and precise command of language with a joyous willingness to measure it against every sort of verbal challenge. Fritz's tendency to distinguish the smallest literary favor with precision and imagination is pat with his tendency to treat even the most fetid and undistinguished humans with a respectful and friendly manner.

One fundamental thesis I offer about Fritz Leiber is simple and compelling. Speaking comprehensively, Fritz Leiber names a phenomenon, an endlessly expanding, interacting, and continuing structure of effects, from the most physical to the most symbolic. It can best be explained by starting with the peculiarities of this particular infant, in this particular environment, and tracing the increasingly psychological and symbolic interchanges between infant and environment. The most concrete and revealing components of this phenomenon, the most lively and most real, are a couple of bookshelves of written work and a man who now lives at 565 Geary Street in San Francisco, who of course is continuing the sorts of symbolic interactions that lead to more books on the shelf. The thesis I offer about Fritz Leiber is simple because it so compactly relates and explains the development of Fritz's life and work in a way that holds up well.

The common sense tale is that of an extremely intelligent and talented young man with a taste for the dramatics without self-revelation, for a language and a life wholly outside his century. But at the same time this man is cripplingly shy, horribly self-conscious, with a sense of guilt and failure, a sense of being out-of-joint with himself and the world that breeds dreams and fantasies. This is a sense which, if strong enough, results in madness. Such a mind can be so afflicted that its sense of itself ruptures, like a space-time-historical continuum so pressed by Snake and Spider activity that it can tell no tale of itself and must fission. This fissioning happens when art and science cannot flex enough, have neither the intellectual creativity nor the courage to hold the reality together. (I must tell you, in this common sense account, that the damage that was written into Fritz's genes or, more likely, the mad and murderous psychological effects of his childhood, are as real as vital statistics. Very clinically, this is someone who has had insomnia, a most reliable indication of psychological trouble, throughout his entire life; and who had—the behavior is the characteristic clinic concomitant—ministered to himself with alcohol and barbituates in a way that equates making oneself happy and putting oneself to sleep. The story is one of agile intelligence, of ego and art, fighting a long-term battle with self-destruction.)

This portrait sees Fritz and his work as he is today. But we read books (works) too. The end casts full illumination through the means,

the earliest scene. Not that the big book of Fritz Leiber is complete—
and that in two ways. First, Fritz has much more work in him. He still
exhausts twenty-year-old fans by walking them around San Francisco.
There is much abrewing: Go, little stories, caper seductively or rau-
cously around his bed—Go, little stories, and fling his fingers on the
typewriter keys. Secondly, Fritz is an artist like the wild old Gully Jim-
son that Alex Guinness plays in *The Horse's Mouth*, whose houseboat
runs the Thames' tide into the Atlantic and transfiguration, while
Gully measures gigantic ocean liners as potential canvasses.

Go little stories, and change the street numbers so the fans can't find
him—fox the postal machines so his mail goes to Auckland, New
Zealand, and viper the wires so that incoming calls move by spidery in-
direction from initial dialing to total confusion. Shake hailstones down
large as spearmint blossoms if he dawdles in the streets or runs unnecessary errands. Sprinkle dust of Yeats and Poe, and toenail clippings of
Robert Graves and Ingmar Bergman, in protective circles round his
rooms. Go, little stories, and pull some strings. Fritz Leiber is for the
stars.

Notes

1. Introduction: The Philosophical Appeal of Science Fiction

1. Isaac Asimov, *I, Robot* (Greenwich, Conn.: Fawcett Crest, 1970). Quoted material from pp. 49, 50, 51, 51, 60, 61.
2. Kate Wilhelm, ed., *Nebula Award Stories Nine* (New York: Bantam, 1978), p. xxiv.
3. Ayn Rand, *The Romantic Manifesto* (New York: Signet, 1971), p. 19.
4. Aristotle, *Poetics* 9, 1451b5–6, translated by Ingram Bywater (Oxford Aristotle).
5. Cf. Rand, *Romantic Manifesto*, pp. 64–66.
6. Robert Scholes and Eric S. Rabkin, *Science Fiction: History, Science, Vision* (Oxford: Oxford University Press, 1977), p. 7.
7. See L. David Allen's superior study, *Science Fiction: An Introduction* (Lincoln, Neb.: Cliff's Notes, 1973) for a statement of this distinction. We are also indebted to Allen for his account of science fiction's presupposition of order.
8. Norman Spinrad, ed., *Modern Science Fiction* (New York: Anchor, 1974), pp. 1–2.
9. Donald C. Williams, "The Myth of Passage," *Journal of Philosophy* 48 (1951), reprinted in Richard M. Gale, ed., *The Philosophy of Time* (New York: Anchor, 1967). J. J. C. Smart makes similar remarks about time travel in his article "Time," in *The Encyclopedia of Philosophy* (New York: Collier Macmillan, 1967).
10. David Lewis, "The Paradoxes of Time Travel," *American Philosophical Quarterly* 13 (1976): 145–52, reprinted in our *Thought Probes*, (Prentice-Hall, 1981).
11. In *New Worlds* (1966), reprinted in Spinrad, *Modern Science Fiction*, and other anthologies. Quoted material from Spinrad, pp. 368, 369, 376f.
12. Thomas Nagel, "What Is It Like to Be a Bat?" *The Philosophical Review* 83, No. 4 (1974): 435–50, reprinted in our *Thought Probes*, (Prentice-Hall, 1981).

195

13. *Intellectual Digest* (1971), reprinted in Thomas E. Sanders, *Speculations* (New York: Glencoe Press, 1973); quoted material from Sanders, pp. 586f., 590.
14. Wilhelm, *Nebula Award Stories Nine.*

3. TIPS FOR TIME TRAVEL

1. The most sophisticated stories of time travel that I have found are Lester Del Rey's ". . . And It Comes Out Here," in *Voyagers in Time,* edited by Robert Silverberg (New York: Grosset & Dunlap, 1967); Robert A. Heinlein, " 'All You Zombies,' " in *The Unpleasant Profession of Jonathan Hoag* (New York: Berkeley Medallion, 1976), reprinted in F. D. Miller and N. D. Smith, *Thought Probes,* (Prentice-Hall, 1981) and "By His Bootstraps," in *The Menace from Earth* (New York: Signet, 1962); and Stanislaw Lem's "The Twentieth Voyage," in *The Star Diaries* (New York: Avon, 1977). The classic tale of time travel, of course, is H. G. Wells' "The Time Machine," in *The Science Fiction Hall of Fame,* Volume IIA, edited by Ben Bova (New York: Avon, 1974).
2. "A Sound of Thunder" is reprinted in Bradbury, *The Golden Apples of the Sun* (New York: Doubleday, 1953).
3. See William Tenn, "Brooklyn Project," in Silverberg, *Voyagers in Time.*
4. See L. Sprague de Camp, "A Gun For Dinosaur," in *3000 Years of Fantasy and Science Fiction,* edited by L. Sprague de Camp and Catherine Crook de Camp (New York: Lothrip, Lee & Shepard, 1972).
5. Compare Jonathan Harrison, "Dr. Who and the Philosophers or Time-Travel for Beginners," *Aristotelian Society,* Supplementary Vol. 45, 1971. Another excellent article that, like Harrison's article, has the virtue of being intelligible to nonphilosophers is David Lewis, "The Paradoxes of Time Travel," *American Philosophical Quarterly,* April 1976, reprinted in F. D. Miller and N. D. Smith, *Thought Probes,* (Prentice-Hall, 1981).
6. Whether one can affect the past (as opposed to changing it) is another problem. There is a large body of literature, both pro and con, discussing whether effects can temporally precede their causes. I shall not enter into this dispute.
7. In Lem's "The Twentieth Voyage," attempts to alter the past fail, but these attempts result in such things as the craters on the moon, the ice ages, and the death of dinosaurs. Nothing is changed, but various facts are explained by the interference of time travellers.
8. Wells, "The Time Machine," p. 459.

4. WILL A RUBBER BALL STILL BOUNCE?

1. For a while, especially in the late sixties, some of what could now pass for mainstream but at the same time nonstandard science fiction was a reflection of some features of the search for alternative realities. In some cases this involved trying to carry new drug-related experiences into the literary effort. It would now be easy to dismiss them and the general hysteria of the Vietnam war years

with a wave of some suitable sociological expression, for the climate has changed and once again grown more conservative. But despite the conservatism, we still find today a major concern to be the fundamental principles of nature that might be other than those of ordinary common sense.

2. Frank Herbert, *Dune* (Philadelphia: Chilton Book Company, 1965).
3. Stephen Donaldson, *The Chronicles of Thomas Covenant the Unbeliever* (New York: Holt, Reinhart, and Winston, 1977).
4. J. R. R. Tolkien, *The Lord of the Rings* (London: George Allen & Unwin, 1956).
5. Robert Silverberg, "In Entropy's Jaws," in *Modern Science Fiction*, edited by N. Spinard (New York: Anchor, 1974).
6. Samuel R. Delaney, *The Einstein Intersection* (New York: Ace Books, 1967).
7. Independent of other criticisms, I find this particular conceit most offensive. It is the most standard of ploys and the least effective. After the unsuccessful conclusion of a quest, the hero always goes off somewhere to refresh his soul! Either Delaney is putting us on here or he has completely given up trying to make his point, for to simply have Lobey wander off into the sunset turns this into a bad Western.
8. See Delaney, p. 127, for an earlier hint at this same point.
9. William Whewell, *Theory of Scientific Method*, edited by R. E. Butts (Pittsburgh: University of Pittsburgh Press, 1968), p. 130.

5. Alternative Linguistic Frameworks

1. Carl Sagan, *Cosmic Connection* (New York: Doubleday, 1973), pp. 217–18.
2. H. Beam Piper, "Omnilingual," in *Mars, We Love You*, edited by Jane Hipolito and Willis E. McNelly (New York: Pyramid, 1971), pp. 257–58.
3. Ibid., p. 259.
4. W. V. Quine, *Word and Object* (Cambridge, Mass.: M.I.T. Press, 1960), p. 70.
5. Ludwig Wittgenstein, *On Certainty*, edited by G. E. M. Anscombe and G. H. Von Wright, translated by Denis Paul and G. E. M. Anscombe (Oxford: Basil Blackwell, 1969), 96. Cf. 94ff.
6. Ibid., 321. Cf. 319–20.
7. W. V. Quine, *From a Logical Point of View*, 2d rev. ed. (New York: Harper & Row, 1961), p. 44.
8. Richard Rorty, "The World Well Lost," *Journal of Philosophy*, 69, No. 19 (October 1972):
9. For a more detailed discussion on the relation of ALF's to human speech and of logic to the world, consult George F. Sefler, *Language and the World* (Atlantic Highlands, N.J.: Humanities Press, 1974), pp. 112–27.

6. Omnilinguals

1. T. S. Kuhn, *The Structure of Scientific Revolutions* (Chicago: University of Chicago Press, 1962). A useful new commentary on Kuhn's ideas is: H. I. Brown,

Perception, Theory, and Commitment (Chicago: University of Chicago Press, 1977). Further developments in the same direction are to be found in I. Lakatos, *The Methodology of Scientific Research Programs*, edited by J. Worral and G. Currie (New York: Cambridge University Press, 1978) and L. Laudan, *Progress and Its Problems; Towards a Theory of Scientific Growth* (Berkeley: University of California Press, 1977).

2. The identification problem may be solved by making contact with an alien culture which evidently possesses a sophisticated technology. Caution: sophisticated technology is no guarantee of intelligence. Two variations on this theme are: Paul Anderson, "Wings of Victory," *Analog*, April 1972, in which human explorers fail to identify intelligent aliens despite their technology, and Larry Niven and Jerry Pournelle, *The Mote in God's Eye* (New York: Simon and Schuster, 1974), wherein human explorers assume incorrectly that the first alien they encounter is intelligent because of its technological accompaniment.

3. The perils of not translating an alien language are underlined by Niven and Pournelle in *The Mote in God's Eye*.

4. Wittgenstein: "If a lion could talk, we could not understand him" (*Philosophical Investigations*, p. 223). The view of translation I am suggesting derives from Wittgenstein rather than Quine or Davidson. According to Wittgenstein, language cannot be treated in isolation from the activities of mankind. The problem of translation is therefore the problem of establishing which activities in a foreign culture correspond to activities in our own. This is why we could not understand the lion. I regret not having space to detail the deficiencies of Quine's position. More of Davidson in note 9.

5. H. Beam Piper, "Omnilingual," *Astounding*, February 1957, pp. 8–46.

6. See note 2.

7. James Blish, *A Case of Conscience* (New York: Ballantine, 1958) p. 21.

8. A. E. Van Vogt, "Far Centaurus," in *Men Against the Stars*, edited by M. Greenburg (New York: Gnome, 1950).

9. Two philosophical disclaimers:

   a. These suggestions in no way conflict with Donald Davidson's well-known demonstration of the impossibility of alternative conceptual schemes. I am not suggesting that the alien scientific theories are untranslatable—only that they will be no easier to translate than anything else. Wittgenstein suggests that understanding can be produced in two ways: by explanation and by training. Davidson's model of translation emphasizes the former. I think that the latter will be much more important in understanding alien languages (see the concluding remarks on first and second language acquisition).

   b. Davidson's argument against Kuhn suggests that Kuhn holds some sort of scheme/content distinction and that this distinction is required to understand scientific revolutions. I doubt that Kuhn ever employed such a distinction, but for my purposes the only relevant feature of scientific revolutions is that they are noncumulative and philosophers as diverse as Kuhn, Lakatos, and Laudan all agree on this.

10. For a detailed defense of the claim that modern mathematics is not a cumulative development from Greek mathematics, see Jacob Klein, *Greek Mathematical*

Thought and the Origin of Algebra, translated by E. Brann (Cambridge, Mass.: MIT Press, 1968), especially chap. 9.

11. Ursula K. Le Guin, *Three Hainish Novels* (New York: Nelson Doubleday, 1977), p. 368.

12. On this point see: Eric H. Lenneberg, *Biological Foundations of Language* (New York: Wiley, 1967).

13. Robert A. Heinlein, *Stranger in a Strange Land* (New York: Putnam, 1961).

14. My thanks to Ian Edward and Dal Coger for bibliographic assistance. I would also like to thank my co-symposiasts at the Popular Culture Association for a number of helpful suggestions.

7. Could Anyone Here Speak Babel-17?

1. Samuel R. Delany, *Babel-17* (New York: Ace Books, 1966), p. 93. It seems unlikely that English will be spoken in its present form so far in the future; but by stipulating that it is, Delany avoids all kinds of problems about world-views and translation that would distract from his main thrust.

2. Ibid., pp. 111, 103, 127–28.

3. Ibid., p. 111. Cf. p. 121.

4. Ibid., pp. 143, 169, 144. See also pp. 127–28.

5. Ibid., pp. 170–71. A special case of the Whorfian hypothesis.

6. Ibid., p. 173.

7. Ibid., pp. 170–71.

8. Ibid., p. 22.

9. Ibid., p. 90. Cf. pp. 56–67 and pp. 112–15. This might sound like a language designed to express the kinds of knowledge characteristic of the right cerebral hemisphere. It must be more than that, however, since it can also handle matters which would require processing by the left hemisphere or both hemispheres.

10. Ibid., pp. 56–57.

11. Ibid., pp. 90, 112–15

12. I have assumed this for the sake of simplicity. The matter is, of course, much more complex. It might be argued that I should be talking about morphemes, since they are, properly speaking, the units of syntax and semantics. At this point, however, the chasm opens. Why morphemes, instead of Chomskian formatives, if we want to talk about the real syntactic units? Do the true syntactic units correspond to semantic units? Chomsky might say yes, but generative semanticists would at least want to qualify any such affirmation. Fascinating as all this is, we can dispense with it here, because the point to be made applies to proper parts of non-picture-languages, regardless of what those parts may be.

13. Delany, *Babel-17*, p. 90.

14. Ibid., pp. 56–57.

15. Ibid.

16. Ibid., pp. 90, 171.

17. Ibid., pp. 143–48, 125, 52. The matter could be argued further. Perhaps the very structure of mind, even when discorporate, acts as a filter. Perhaps telepathy is *not* direct perception. However, I doubt that further torture of the text will produce a view that can be better supported by it than the one I have presented, since as far as I can tell Delany does not address the questions raised in this note.
18. Ibid., p. 173.
19. Ibid., pp. 122–23.
20. Ibid., p. 173.

8. WHO INHABITS RIVERWORLD?

1. Philip Jose Farmer's "Riverworld" series consists (so far) of *To Your Scattered Bodies Go* (New York: Berkeley, 1971), *The Fabulous Riverboat* (New York: Berkeley, 1973), *The Dark Design* (New York: Berkeley, 1977), and *The Magic Labyrinth* (New York: Berkeley, 1980). A precursor of the series is "Riverworld," in P. J. Farmer, *Down in the Black Gang* (Garden City, N.Y.: Nelson Doubleday, 1971).
2. Farmer, *To Your Scattered Bodies Go*, pp. 139–41.
3. Farmer, *Magic Labyrinth*, p. 307.
4. Cf. Bernard Williams, "The Self and the Future," in *Personal Identity*, edited by John Perry (Berkeley: University of California Press, 1975).
5. Farmer, *Magic Labyrinth*, pp. 302–8.
6. Ibid. p. 307.

9. MULTIPLE SELVES AND SURVIVAL OF BRAIN DEATH

1. In pursuing this analysis I have waived important questions about the adequacy of bundle theories for preserving important features of our ordinary way of looking at ourselves, namely our usual belief that we have some sort of persisting identity over time such that my present experiences occur to the same self as my past ones did, and our usual belief that I have some legitimate personal (existential) concern for my own future states. I have serious doubts about physicalism on this score, and believe Hume was right. Unless there is some sort of substantial mentalist self, our normal beliefs in self-identity have no real ground.
2. These problems have been explored in many papers. Two particularly valuable treatments are found in Terence Penelhum, *Survival and Disembodied Existence* (London: Routledge and Kegan Paul, 1970), and Antony Flew, *The Presumption of Atheism* (London: Elek Books, 1976). Neither Flew nor Penelhum agrees with my conclusions and neither in fact accepts physicalism as I have described it. Both are "ordinary language" philosophers and reject the physicalism (central–state materialism) that I am discussing. Also, it must be noted that I

have assumed a Humean sort of "bundle" theory of self and that there may be central-state materialists who reject that notion. The concept (self-transplant) that I have adopted makes sense with a bundle theory and the resolutions I urge work with that theory.

3. Lest it be thought that the Scheffing process is not really possible, what about the literature on multiple personality? The "three faces" of Eve seemed to be able to interact in the ways Silverberg requires. How the physiology works is unknown, but it seems reasonable to suppose that if multiple personalities can be produced "naturally" they can also be produced "artificially."

4. If you are convinced, as I am, that bundle theories can handle neither self-identity nor my concern for my future selves, then you have to engage in criticism of both science-fiction accounts. Neither account works if mentalism is true, and I am convinced that mentalism is required to support our usual beliefs about self-identity and our relations to our own future states. In my opinion bundle theories would not justify either a person's regarding her own future states as genuinely hers or regarding her past states as genuinely hers. For the sake of analysis I have assumed that bundle theories can handle that common-sense sense of identity over time.

5. In an earlier note I have indicated an alternative analysis. I am here assuming that Silverberg is correct that successor selves should be regarded as the same self as the preduplicated self by the preduplicated self. I do not really think that bundle theories justify that common sense belief that I should really be concerned about my successor states. We could also go the other way and deny that either novel has it right when it assumes that duplicates are the same as their originals or that successor selves are the same as their duplicate predecessors. We could take a Humean view and deny that identity ever holds between successive selves in any strict sense.

10. THE COALESCENCE OF MINDS

1. Arthur C. Clarke, *Childhood's End* (New York: Ballantine, 1953), p. 184.

2. Pierre Teilhard de Chardin, *The Phenomenon of Man* (New York: Harper & Row, 1959), p. 92.

3. Pierre Teilhard de Chardin, *The Future of Man* (New York: Pyramid Books, 1966), p. 164.

4. Ibid., p. 116.

5. Olaf Stapledon, *Last and First Men* (New York: Dover, 1968), pp. 34, 231.

6. John Dewey, *Experience and Nature* (New York: Dover, 1958), pp. 258, 261.

7. See, for example, Edward E. Smith, *First Lensman* (New York: Pyramid Books, 1971). Full telepathic rapport is "more intimate than a kiss," and "mental communication, so much clearer and faster than physical" is possible "without the laborious learning of language." Telepathic thoughts "come from the mind itself, direct, not through such voluntary muscles as the tongue" (pp. 23, 92, 218, 43, 65). There is here a typical confusion between the physical character of sounds or marks and their use.

8. John Dewey, *Experience and Nature*, pp. 256, 292. See also Kurt Goldstein, *The Organism* (Boston: Beacon Press, 1963), pp. 34–35. C. H. Waddington's *The Ethical Animal* (Chicago: University of Chicago Press, 1967), esp. chap. 9, "The Biological Evolutionary System," is also of interest in this connection.

9. Edward E. Smith, *Children of the Lens* (New York: Pyramid Books, 1967), p. 172. See also Floyd Allport, "Logical Complexities of Group Activity," in *Philosophical Problems of the Social Sciences*, edited by David Braubrooke (New York: Macmillan, 1965).

10. Stapledon, *Last and First Men*, p. 224.

11. Ibid., p. 222.

12. Pierre Teilhard de Chardin, *Human Energy* (New York: Harcourt Brace Jovanovich, 1969), pp. 72–74. See also Teilhard de Chardin, *Future of Man*, p. 124.

13. Teilhard de Chardin, *Future of Man*, p. 98.

14. Stapledon, *Last and First Men*, p. 212. See also pp. 232–33.

II. THE ELUSIVE SELF AND THE INTIMIDATING OTHER

1. This problem set is quite complex. A thorough philosophical analysis and explication would have to include an extended treatment, carefully distinguishing and dealing with each of the many aspects, and then developing their logical interrelationships, as well as showing the strengths and weaknesses involved and the implications and consequences that follow. My goals in this paper are more modest and limited.

2. Positive reinforcement, it is said, provides a more efficient and effective conditioning of desired behavior and extinction of unwanted behavior than does negative reinforcement or "punishment"; the proving ground is with "animals," the extrapolation is to "the human animal."

3. The machine model reaches back in "modern" thought at least as far as Descartes, or to a half of Descartes. Perhaps René Descartes has been given too much credit (translated: unforgiving blame) for "cursing modern man" with both the mechanistic interpretation of the body and the mind-body split. There may well be other factors which retain and strengthen the hold of this model upon modern humans.

4. Cf., for example, John Burke's "The Wheel of Fortune," BBC film (broadcast over PBS, WWVU-TV, November 3, 1979), in which it is indicated that that which made achievement and industrial progress possible also resulted in loss of individualism, i.e., in being all essentially alike, wanting, having, consuming the same things, we thereby become "the same." For both a criticism of "single vision" and hope, see Theodore Roszak, *Where the Wasteland Ends: Politics and Transcendence in Postindustrial Society* (Garden City, N.Y.: Doubleday, Anchor, 1973). A not totally inaccurate gauge to the popularity of both of these models and their variations may be the number of paperback books and magazine arti-

cles which are "consumed" (written, published and sold/bought) and which make their promise and have their appeal apparently on the adoption of one or the other of these models as "solutions" to our problems. As noted, specialists use the models, too.

5. Isaac Asimov, *I, Robot* (Greenwich, Conn.: Fawcett, Crest, 1970), pp. 147–70.
6. Jack Williamson, *The Best of Jack Williamson* (New York: Ballantine Books, 1978), pp. 154–206.
7. Included in Leslie A. Fielder, *In Dreams Awake* (New York: Dell, 1975), pp. 289–315.
8. Asimov's invention; these Laws have, by and large, ruled the robot stories since Asimov introduced them in the field.
9. Asimov, *I. Robot*, p. 158.
10. Ibid., p. 6.
11. Ibid., p. 158.
12. Ibid., p. 159.
13. Ibid., pp. 169–70.
14. Ibid., p. 170.
15. Williamson, *The Best of Jack Williamson*, p. 170.
16. Ibid. pp. 205–6.
17. Perhaps we have ample evidence of such connection through persons' experiences within our society currently, e.g., forced retirement or some not knowing what to do if they retire from their jobs, and also in cases of significant changes in vocational opportunities or directions.
18. Fielder's *In Dreams Awake*, p. 290.
19. Ibid., pp. 314–15.

12. ABSURDITY OF SARTRE'S ONTOLOGY

1. Ursula K. Le Guin, "A Trip to the Head," *The Wind's Twelve Quarters* (London: Victor Gollancz Ltd., 1976), pp. 173–80.
2. Jean-Paul Sartre, *Being and Nothingness*, translated by Hazel E. Barnes (New York: Washington Square Press, 1953).
3. Ibid., pp. 24–30.
4. Ibid., pp.7–9.
5. Jean-Paul Sartre, *Nausea*, translated by Lloyd Alexander (Norfolk, Conn.: New Directions, 1959), p. 171.
6. Sartre, *Being and Nothingness*, pp. 119–55.
7. Ibid., pp. 301–401.
8. Ibid., pp. 340–401.
9. Le Guin, "A Trip to the Head," pp. 173–80.
10. Ibid., p. 174.
11. Ibid., pp. 179–80.

13. GROKKING THE STRANGER

1. Robert A. Heinlein, *Stranger in a Strange Land,* (New York: Berkeley, 1961), p. 46.
2. Ibid., p. 84.
3. Ibid., p. 85.
4. Ibid.
5. Ibid., p. 80.
6. Ibid., p. 85.
7. Ibid., p. 86.
8. Ibid., p. 84.
9. Both the Martian "Old Ones" and the ritual of sharing water have been established features of Heinlein's fiction since his *Red Planet* in 1949. Usually his Martians are equipped with supranormal mental powers, and this is certainly the case in *Stranger.*
10. Heinlein, *Stranger,* p. 69.
11. Ibid., p. 115.
12. Ibid., pp. 147–48.
13. Ibid., p. 137.
14. Ibid., p. 65.
15. Ibid., p. 393.
16. Ibid., p. 65.
17. Ibid., p. 299, 300.
18. Ibid., p. 300.
19. Damon Knight, "One Sane Man: Robert A. Heinlein," in *In Search of Wonder* (Chicago: Advent, 1967), pp. 83–84, 86.
20. David N. Samuelson, "The Frontier Worlds of Robert A. Heinlein," in *Voices for the Future,* vol. 1, edited by Clareson (Bowling Green, Ohio: Bowling Green University Press, 1976), p. 140.
21. Frank Herbert, *Dune,* (New York: Ace, 1965), p. 98.
22. Kurt Vonnegut, Jr., *Breakfast of Champions* (New York: Dell n.d.), p. 198.
23. Tom Wolfe, *The Electric Kool-Aid Acid Test* (New York: Bantam, 1968), p. 123.